BIS Publishers
Building Het Sieraad
Postjesweg 1
1057 DT Amsterdam
The Netherlands
bis@bispublishers.com
www.bispublishers.com

CREATIVE PERSONAL BRANDING

All web references were correct at the time of going to press.

ISBN 978 90 6369 315 2
Category: Education / Personal / Marketing

Editor: Vicky Hayward
Book Designer: Simon Hüsler
Copy Editor: Anna Bennett

Copyright © 2013 Jürgen Salenbacher and BIS Publishers
5th printing 2018

THE STRATEGY TO ANSWER
WHAT'S NEXT?

CREATIVE

CREATE OPPORTUNITIES

PERSONAL

GROW PERSONALLY

BRANDING

DIFFERENTIATE YOURSELF

JÜRGEN SALENBACHER

Thanks to my beloved wife Carina. ¡te quiero muchisimo!

OPPORTUNITY FAVOURS
THE PREPARED MIND!

REFRESH

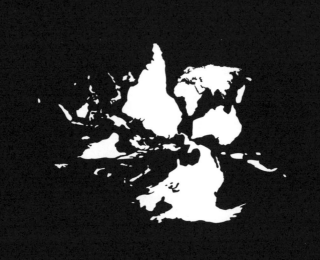

THE WORLD CHANGES
AND WE MUST
CHANGE WITH IT!

Barack Obama, President of the United States

CPB
CONTENTS

The CPB Process At A Glance

01
REFLECT!

What The Hell Is Going On?

02
REFRAME!

Positive Thinking / New Skills

03
CREATE!

How To Create Opportunities

04
GROW!

How To Grow Personally

05
DIFFERENTIATE!

How To Differentiate

06
GO!

Where Next?

PREFACE — HOW TO ENJOY THIS BOOK

We live in a state of *constant flux*. Industries, markets, companies, competitors and customers change. Countries rise, others disappear – companies and brands too. That has always happened throughout history but the speed of change over the last twenty years, ever since the Internet entered our life and reduced distance, time and cost, has been tremendous.

What are the consequences for the individual? Well, we now have total competition with a lower margin for error in a more complex and ever-changing professional environment. It seems paradoxical that we have more choices than ever before, but I don't see people being any happier. What I see is a *collective insecurity*. Many people I know of different ages, genders, educational background and levels of experience have either been laid off or are required to do unsustainable hours of work to maintain their standard of living. Students now tend to do two degrees, hoping that this will guarantee them future success. Everything and everyone seems to be in a *state of limbo*, a strange transition between the past and the future. I call it the limbo-generation. Everybody is facing the same question: 'What should I do next?'

I want to share with you my strategy for answering this question: **Creative Personal Branding**. Its four key values are substance, style, conviction and grace. It aims to develop *creative leadership*, helping you to identify *where* to go, *how* to get there and with *whom*.

This book explains its methodology as I have developed it over the last decade:

1. Learning the importance of creativity and *creative thinking*, to identify or create opportunities, focusing on new ways of thinking that are environmentally, financially and socially sustainable.
2. Understanding the importance of what you have to offer the world, *your role*, your expertise and passion, your integrity of vision and mission and your values.
3. Understanding the importance of the *brand-positioning method* to differentiate and communicate yourself on- and offline in the age of connectivity and online reputation.

The outcome?

A bright and exciting vision of your future. What more can you expect? Don't expect this book to solve all your problems, however. Its intention instead is to motivate and inspire you by encouraging your creative thinking to develop a sense of direction, brand strategy and social networks which suit your unique personality. Inspirational ideas for a short trip with long-lasting impact.

A few last comments on how to enjoy this book. It refers to examples that describe the change I have seen and the insights I gained working as a designer, marketing and strategy director, as well as teacher and coach over the last twenty years. You can just read it – but if you want to get the most out of it I strongly recommend that you answer the questions and carry out the assignments given at the end of each section. They give you a starting point and a structured approach to developing your strategy for your future in the creative economy and answering what's next.

In the introductory first chapter you will reflect on change in the recent past and estimate relevant tendencies for the near future. In the second chapter, you will look at ways of reframing work opportunities. The third chapter, on creativity, lets you discover how to identify opportunities and think about ideas, especially your best business idea. In the fourth chapter, on personality, you will find methods and assignments to discover your potential and define your vision and mission as well as your goals and objectives – all these value-led. In the fifth chapter, on branding, you will also get a structured approach on how to develop your visual identity on- and offline and, as always, how and where to apply it. Then there is the Creative Personal Branding manifesto, some extra ideas in the notes and a short list of my most valued reading.

Above all, though, *enjoy!*

A JOURNEY FROM UNCERTAINTY
TO A NEW VISION

Creative Personal Branding aims to develop creative leadership, helping you to identify where to go, how to get there and with whom.

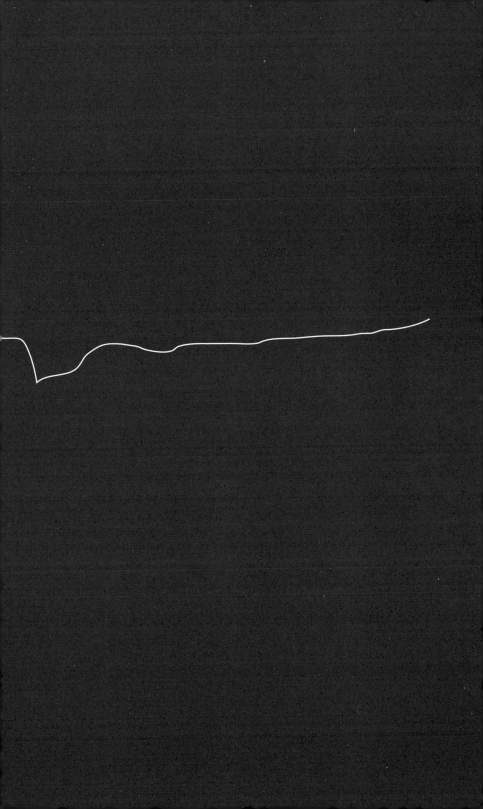

01
_REFLECT!

What The Hell Is Going On?

WHAT THE HELL IS GOING ON?

Most of us don't like change. Why? Because it means making an effort to move out of our perceived *comfort zones*. Very often change also brings uncertainty with it. Few see opportunities. Many are paralysed, disorientated or confused by lack of stability or too many options. Life today is like a hypermarket with about an average of 70,000 products stocked on the shelves.[1] You enter a shop because you want to buy an apple, and you end up buying a banana. Who knows why?

Of course your reaction to change depends on where you are in life. You may be a student, unemployed, an entrepreneur, a freelancer or a company manager. Ever-increasing responsibilities such as family and children, a mortgage or employees may seem to make it impossible to change. They leave us exhausted at the end of the day. These responsibilities are in many cases the principal reasons for people putting up with the same situation, the same job, the same company for years on end. This continues until one day the environment forces us to change, pushing us. God alone knows whether towards good or bad.

'The world changes, and we must change with it.' There was nothing new about the words Barack Obama used on 20 January 2009. What was new was Obama's attitude towards change: **'Yes, we can.'**

Taking this as a premise, wouldn't it be better to prepare ourselves and take the initiative in embracing change in our lives instead of being changed by others? To take a positive attitude towards change? To see the exciting opportunities it offers, rather than just the threats? Personally I don't like other people taking decisions in my life – I prefer to take them on my own, for better

LIFE TODAY IS LIKE A HYPERMARKET.

*You enter a shop because you want to buy an apple, and you end up buying a banana. **Who knows why?***

or worse. But at least I can stop blaming others. This saves a lot of time and energy which is far more enjoyably invested writing on an exciting new blank page: **my future!**

THE FORCE OF CHANGE: LIFE AT SPEED

What the hell is going on? That was the first question I asked myself when I started work on this book, just as the biggest economic crisis since the Great Depression of 1929 was unfolding. Like many others, I felt strange about the impacts of the financial crisis, economic instability and the tremendous job losses in the USA and Europe. When a company such as Lehman Brothers went bankrupt in 2008 I was really surprised. A company with 128 years of history – a company which had survived Black Friday in 1929 and two world wars. Then we heard about countries like Iceland on the point of bankruptcy. Later still, Dubai was in serious financial trouble and so too Ireland, Greece, Portugal, Spain … and we still do not know where it will end.

All that has happened in just ten years since the last recession in 2001. Not long ago. And, be sure, the next recession will not be too far away.

The key point is that these are not just events happening somewhere else. We read about those in the *Financial Times* or watching CNN. We feel touched by them, somehow, but they are of no further personal consequence to us. No, this is the real news, which affects us all, more then ever before. Especially our work and lives – yours and mine. We still receive daily news about historic companies closing down and widespread job losses. An extreme case is Spain, where, at the end of 2012, unemployment reached 26,6% and even 56,5% among people under 25, according to *Eurostat*.[2]

Whatever you read or watch, the key message is always the same: change is a fact of life. One of the key Buddhist beliefs is that everything changes. History is full of change. But today it seems our economy and, therefore, our society is affected by a new form of change, something more radical and faster than ever before. And the most visible sign of change is clearly defined: nothing is long-term. **Work and life seem to change at a pace never seen before.** If you are confused, have doubts or are sometimes frustrated by this, you are definitely not alone. In *Spaceballs*, the science fiction parody of *Star Wars* (starwars.com), there were four levels of speed: sub-light, light, ridiculous and ludicrous. We are already working at a *ridiculous speed*. No wonder so many of us are confused.

OK, but what is new that makes today's change so important? How does change affect our economy and our society today and in the future? What are the consequences for the individual? For our future work and life? Our education and career? How can we prepare and adapt? Most important of all, how can we develop a strategy to answer 'what's next'?

WWW: THE WORLD CUP …

I felt I needed to look back to understand what is influencing our changing lives in such a profound way. Within only a few months in the year 1990, I found a constellation of three clustered events, each symbolising a different aspect of the nature of that change.

In 1990 I was twenty years old and ready to set the world on fire during a beautiful hot summer in my home region in southwest Germany. This was the year of the World Cup, the Pink Floyd concert 'The Wall' and the Web.

The World Cup final: 8 July 1990. Germany beat Argentina in Rome: 1:0. That was the good part. According to ESPN soccernet, however, this was 'one of the poorest World Cups ever'. The final was described by veteran football writer Brian Glanville as 'probably the worst, most tedious, bad-tempered final in the history of the World Cup.'

Why so? Well, it generated a record low goals-per-game average, and sixteen red cards, then a record, were handed out. Most teams relied heavily on defensive play and hard tackling. What was the reason for that defensive strategy? Defending their status from whom? What makes teams like Germany and Italy try to play safe and more roughly than before?

Looking back, it seems that those teams tried to defend their market share as more new competition came into the market place. Does that make sense? To flesh it out, in the 1990 World Cup African countries like Cameroon entered the world stage and ended up as quarter-finalists for the first time. It was the last time we saw Yugoslavia and Czechoslovakia as teams: their players were to come back under re-named teams.

Since then the tournament has continued to expand: from sixteen teams in 1978 to thirty-two in 1998, allowing more teams from Asia, Africa and North America to take part. Imagine only that 204 teams attempted to qualify for the 2010 FIFA World Cup.[3] The results, too, have been astonishing. Senegal and USA were both quarter-finalists in 2001, and South Korea finished in fourth place at the same year. So, while the game and rules have not changed, change has come through everyone wanting to participate with formerly unknown nations, now much better prepared, gaining a market share. That has upset traditionally successful nations and may make them play more aggressively.

The fact is: there is now much more competition on a global level. And, of course – which is why I am telling you this story – not only at the World Cup.

WWW: ... 'THE WALL' ...

Just thirteen days after the World Cup final, on 21 July 1990, I saw Roger Waters of Pink Floyd play to 350,000 people at the Potsdamer Platz in Berlin at the famous concert called 'The Wall'. It was a warm Saturday night, charged with emotion. This was the first time after forty years of separation that people from east and west came together to celebrate the tearing down of the Berlin Wall on its former no-man's land. That magic moment had a tremendous and long-lasting political, geographical and ideological impact.

Think about the world map. Borders move constantly. They change so fast it is almost impossible, even for someone who is travelling a lot, to draw a correct map of their actual status. The European Union, for example, has grown to include more than twenty new nations since the Wall fell: they now include Slovakia, Slovenia and Bulgaria. We have in recent years seen countries like East Germany, Yugoslavia, Czechoslovakia and the Soviet Union merge or split and the *BRIC* countries (Brazil, Russia, India and China) and South Korea emerge.

As borders move constantly and become more flexible, they also become more open to trade and investment, and this increases global trade. The World Trade Organization (wto.org), which, with its 158 member states, represents around 97% of the world trade, says that since 1950 world trade has grown more than twenty-seven fold in volume terms. The share of international trade in world GDP (gross domestic product – the basic measure of a country's overall economic output in a year) has risen from 5.5% in 1950 to 20.5% in 2006.[4] Just to give you an idea, developing countries today are responsible for 26% of world exports, which is double their output in the 1960s, but that is still not a lot if you think that the BRIC countries and South Korea alone account for half of the world's population of 7 billion people.

All of this is proof of the extent to which falling walls and more flexible boundaries are helping to bring about a global trade expansion.

WWW: ... AND THE WEB

Another five months and four days later, on 25 December 1990, Tim Berners-Lee (w3.org/People/Berners-Lee/) established the first communication between an HTTP client and server via the Internet.

That first Internet connection was the official start of real change in how we communicate, do business, work and live. After physical and ideological boundaries became more flexible, technology helped us to make boundaries virtually non-existent and magnified the effect of a global world. Instead of east meeting west, everyone now meets everyone. On the one hand the entry barrier was lowered in almost all the markets, and the costs for searching for any kind of provider dropped to almost zero. On the other hand the access to information and knowledge began to come at a speed never experienced before. The Internet connection was the *springboard* for our knowledge industry, 'an industry where success depends on obtaining, managing, and using knowledge in a particular area', according to the *Financial Times* (lexicon.ft.com).

I wouldn't limit the definition only to 'a particular area', however. Success depends on managing knowledge in any area and, more importantly, if you are logged on, anywhere and anytime.

CONNECTIVITY: THE SPRINGBOARD

Looking back at those three events, clustered within a few months in 1990, they still stand as markers for the take-off of connectivity at a pace never seen before. Whenever and wherever, choice rules.

Dave Evans, Cisco (cisco.com) futurologist – an amazing job title, by the way – has talked about an exponential growth of technology and information, which according to him will lead to an accelerated rate of innovation. He sees it as a *technology avalanche* – or you could see it as a wave. You either surf it or you get crushed under it. Evans says that nowadays the volume of information doubles every 11 hours, but less than ten years from now it will double every 11 seconds.[5] As data storage goes up and costs go down, and more people connect to the net and therefore have the best chance ever to get a good education, innovation will be seen in all areas of life.

Connectivity, then, is the springboard to change, which

is bringing much higher participation from more countries, cultures and mentalities as boundaries fall. Connectivity is also about bridging borders, as technology makes information accessible to everyone almost everywhere. For a few years now I have been working with service providers from Argentina, Brazil, Turkey and India. I find they work faster, more cheaply and usually more reliably than European providers do. So why would I not take advantage of that?

But who is actually connected? Who is online? The answer is even more interesting than the question. Tracking global Internet usage I found that 2.4 billion people – around 34,3% of the world population – were online. Of those 44,8% are from Asia, 21,5% from Europe, 11,4% from North America, 10,6% from Latin America, 7% from Africa, 3,7% from the Middle East and 1% from Australia.[6] I repeat, among all Internet users only 21,5% are from Europe and only 11,4% from North America.

Of course Asia's leading position reflects how many people live in that continent, but its high participation favours its ability to innovate, disseminate knowledge and distribute goods and services online. Knowing that the global demand for information and communication technologies is a market worth € 2000 billion[7], I am not that surprised to find Europe is not in a top position. **With 44,8% of Internet users coming from Asia, a massive work- and sales force has now direct access to the European and American markets.** And these are not only cheap and poor-quality imitations. China overtook Japan as the world's second largest economy in the first quarter of 2010, almost a full decade before most expected this to happen, and is expected to be the largest producer of scientific knowledge by 2020. These are just two examples of change which is having a major impact on companies and ultimately on the individual.

THE GLOBAL MARKET: WHENEVER, WHEREVER, CHOICE RULES!

Through connectivity at a pace never seen before!
But who is connected?

Assignment — 1:
WHAT'S NEXT? IDENTIFY THREE RELEVANT TENDENCIES IN YOUR MARKET

The following exercise is the basis for answering the question: what's next? Start with your own reality, past and future. Be precise and go into details. Search for numbers and statistics.

My personal suggestion This isn't an easy assignment, I know, but it's well worth doing. Talk to other people, exchange ideas, read articles, analyse, synthesise and write everything down. A few years ago I found myself stuck, unfocused and without markets in which to grow. After carrying out this assignment, applying it to new industries where I could spread my knowledge, I came up with several markets, including healthcare, education and energy. So for me it worked well.

1 — Reflect:

a) On the three most important changes in your industry and in your market over the last fifteen years.

_____

_____

_____

_____

_____

b) On the changes you predict will happen in the next fifteen years.

_____

_____

_____

_____

_____

c) Think about any threats and opportunities that will affect your industry and therefore your aims.

_____

_____

_____

_____

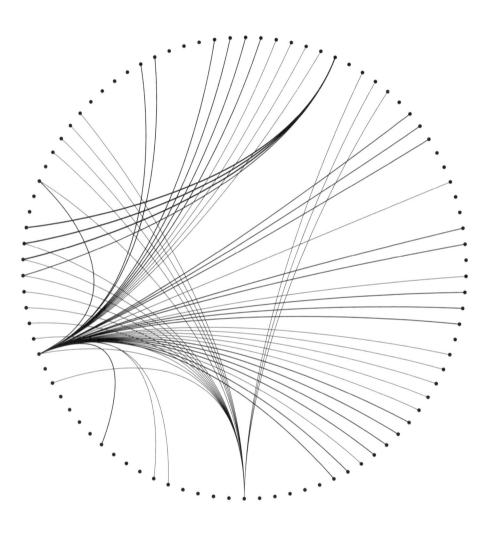

02
_REFRAME!

Positive Thinking / New Skills

POSITIVE THINKING / NEW SKILLS

Companies' behaviour is not so very different from that of people. If companies, for example, feel change is a threat rather than an opportunity, they may flee, fight or become paralysed. The fact is business moves forward, however. We will not stop change. Nor should we want to. The human race is able to adapt to new environments. Charles Darwin expressed it well: 'It is not the strongest of the species that survive, nor the most intelligent that survives. It is the one that is the most adaptable to change.'

Nowadays developing countries, for example in Asia, are often more ready to adapt than European ones, not only because they are more responsive, but because they are enthusiastic to create a brighter future. I had a fortune cookie the other day saying 'a man without a smiling face shouldn't open a shop'. Right! In Chinese, the word 'crisis' has two characters: danger and opportunity. If you see *opportunity*, you feel optimistic. If you combine that with the Chinese Mandarin translation – and understanding - of the World Wide Web as a *'myriad dimensional net'* you can see why the Chinese attitude helps them look for, and find, opportunity in change. Yet so often in the west we see change as a threat.

To keep calm when under threat, it is said, you need to observe and plan. Easily said, but imagine you are facing a King Brown snake in the Australian outback and you have a phobia about snakes. You just want to run away. I know. I found myself in that very situation some years ago. Why do we want to run? The sense of threat makes the blood flow to our feet, and so we start to run away, or it may flow to our arms and they start fighting, or to our stomach, which makes our belly hurt and we feel paralysed and stop moving.

A MAN WITHOUT A SMILING FACE SHOULDN'T OPEN A SHOP!

Fortune cookie

Do any of these three experiences sound familiar? The key to them all is where the blood comes from. Our brain weighs only 2% of our total weight, but contains 25% blood. The blood which flows to your arms, legs or stomach, therefore, obviously comes from your brain. You need blood in your brain at those moments for the brain to be able to support your skill in observing, evaluating and planning opportunities and solutions. What would you do, then, faced by the King Brown snake? I'll tell you what I did. I tried to stand still and hoped not to scare it to try to avoid it feeling threatened and defending itself as best as it can. **We need to bear that in mind as we, too, face change: treat change with respect and react with common sense, positive thinking and creative spontaneity.** Think first before you move and especially before you run away.

We, too, need to lead change. We need new skills to identify opportunities and we need to combine creative and business thinking to come up with innovation. We need to keep the blood flowing through our brain.

CREATIVE AND BUSINESS THINKING

The impact of technology-based change on our lives since Tim Berners-Lee invented the World Wide Web in 1990 has been tremendous. I sometimes tell my students that the impact of the technological revolution on our society seems to me much greater than that of the French Revolution. That revolution was of huge importance in shaping modern western democracy. Today's digital revolution will be of enormous importance in shaping a future democracy with a global scope. **Bits and bytes, combined with ideas, give real power to the people, though it may take another fifty years for us to understand this fully.**

That is why I am surprised to hear how politicians so often treat, and talk of, today's crisis as if it was a series of short-term problems instead of a much more complex *structural long-term change*. They talk about how to get out of this crisis, but scarcely mention how to prevent the next one. What I want to look at instead is how the rapidly changing environment of our brand new economy offers many opportunities for us – but, if you are not prepared for it, how it represents a great deal of threat.

Here are some examples of companies which have found opportunity through new business models.

Nike (nike.com) changed its business model some years ago. It is not a manufacturer any more, but mainly a marketing company. Nike develops its marketing, design and branding strategy within the company, but production is outsourced and carried out in the cheapest place. Nike's competitive edge is its ideology. With fewer fixed costs the company can focus on ideas and innovation, and come up with concepts such as NIKE iD. (nikeid.nike.com), a website that transforms the visitor into a designer with the possibility of customising his or her own footwear or gear.

Another example is Lego (lego.com). When Lego was in a downturn it sold off one of its fixed assets, the Legoland theme parks, to keep costs down. It sounds strange for a branding and marketing expert to sell a core piece of the brand, one which lets people experience the brand concept – *'play'* – to its fullest. At that time the company was under immense pressure because of new competitors and copycats, however, and the sale allowed it to survive. After adapting to the new reality, Lego is now back on track.

BITS AND BYTES, COMBINED WITH IDEAS, GIVE REAL POWER TO THE PEOPLE.

*Today's digital revolution will be of enormous importance in **shaping a future democracy** with global scope.*

Another strategy for companies is to buy other companies – or competitors – to increase their market share and presence in different markets, to gain knowledge and patents, optimise human capital and, ultimately, to make business more profitable. Consulting company Accenture works on this principle. In the global economy cross-border *M&As* (mergers and acquisitions) are a key strategy in the pursuit of high performance; these kinds of strategies, to redefine the business model by using technology and optimising costs, will continue. Ideas and innovation are key factors, and technology enables us to test these innovations in reality. If they work it is easy to scale them virtually and then, if necessary, to buy local companies to adapt a virtual model to a new market. This new reality challenges all industries and markets.

Google (google.com) has created a *benchmark* for the traditional advertising industry. With just 25% of the staff of the second player in its market Google makes double the revenue and increase its profits fourfold. How will the advertising industry react? No doubt they will come up with an idea – the industry is full of smart people with great ideas - but they now need to rethink their business model and until they have found a solution they will keep reducing their fixed costs to be more flexible. Google, meanwhile, keeps innovating and enters new industries. Let's wait and see whether and how Google continues to innovate. The results of their past innovations have been impressive. Google Trends, Google Docs and Google Maps are already accepted by the market. Other ideas, like Google Glasses, Google Goggles and Google Mars are very cool, but we consumers have yet to decide if they will work. In any case, and this is the main point, while others talk about innovation, Google innovates, invests resources and is not afraid to fail.

Next, think about the fashion industry. I expect you are already aware of how H&M, or Hennes & Mauritz (hm.com), founded in 1947, Zara (zara.com) and Mango (mango.com) changed the industry just a decade ago by increasing *speed to market* so rapidly that most competitors just could not keep up. What's next in the fast fashion business? Yoox (yoox.com), founded in 2000, just a few weeks after the demise of *boo.com*[1], the mother of all online fashion retailers, spotted a gap in the fashion market where the norm is an abundance of product, and speed and the trends are must-dos for the market leaders. Yoox now offers stocks and unsold items of top brands from previous seasons and sells them with a significant price reduction online to their steadily increasing client base. In ten years it has grown from nothing to a $138-million turnover company with eighty employees. This is nothing, perhaps, in comparison with H&M's $11 billion turnover, but H&M needs 78,000 people to achieve this. **The key question is: who is more flexible in the face of further change and new opportunities?** Beside that, Yoox license their online store system, which they have developed themselves, to many of their clients, from Armani to Stone Island. Their business strategy: be part of the industry's value chain and create a real sustainable competitive advantage through technology.

Never underestimate the changes brought about by technology and connectivity. The first commercially successful camera film, *Kodachrome*, the one I always bought when I was a design student, has disappeared from the market after seventy-four years. Brands like Agfa, Konica and Eastman-Kodak had to go through tough years with their photo-imaging divisions, some of which have now been relegated to history. Most photographic companies underestimated the power and especially the pace of how digital technology could change the market and consumer habits. Kodak (kodak.com), for example, went down from 145,000 employees in 1997 to just 20,000 today.[2] The company patented the basic technologies for digital photography in 1975, but didn't know how to take advantage of this opportunity.

They could have learnt from the Swiss watch industry. In 1968 this controlled around 90% of the global watch market. The consortium responsible assigned a couple of engineers to investigate how the watch of the future could be made. The engineers came back and presented a digital watch right in time for the annual Geneva watch exhibition. The consortium was so disappointed and angry about what, in their opinion, was a useless and cheap proposal that they sent the engineers straight back home together with the copyrights on their designs. The engineers, frustrated, decided to show their designs independently at the exhibition, Japanese companies came along to their stand and were so interested they bought the rights on the spot. The rest is history. The consequence of the Swiss watch industry turning down the digital watch? In a mere ten years this went down from 90% to around 10% of the market share. It took them decades to gain a share of the market back.

CREATIVE ECONOMY: GLOBAL REALITY

If we go one step further in looking at the patterns in this exponential growth in global trade we can see another strong tendency, this time towards a service-orientated world economy of companies that earn revenue primarily through intangible products and services such as accounting, banking, cleaning, computing, consulting, education, insurance or medical treatment and transportation, to name a few. Since 1990, according to The United Nations' Conference on Trade and Development (unctad.org), world trade in services has more than tripled, accounting for 71% of global GDP in 2010.

Within this clear trend towards service there is a second tendency: towards creative services such as design, marketing, software development or entertainment. How large their role is can be seen by comparing the growth rate of total world exports of conventional services between 2000 and 2008, which rose about 13.5% annually, to the annually growth of 17% rate of creative services such as advertising, architecture or audiovisual services in the same period.[3] These figures reflect a shift towards a service-orientated and knowledge-based economy based on *individuals' creativity* in using accessible information to benefit and create values for themselves and others.

This new economy links culture and society, technology and economy, both on macro and micro levels. Central to its paradigm is the recognition that creativity, knowledge and access to information are powerful engines for driving economic growth and promoting development in a globalising world. **This, again, is something new: we are starting to value creativity.** One single idea has the power to make a company's business grow. The *ROC (return on creativity)* can be tremendous. Creativity and the capability to innovate, in other words to apply ideas in a business context, seems to be a key component of this *creative economy* emerging in the twenty-first century.

The United Nations' Conference on Trade and Development *Creative Economy Report 2010* defined the emerging 'creative economy' as:

- an evolving concept based on creative assets
- potentially generating economic growth and development
- holding the potential to foster income generation, job creation and export earnings while promoting social inclusion, cultural diversity and human development
- embracing economic, cultural and social aspects interacting with technology, intellectual property and tourism
- a set of knowledge-based economic activities with a development dimension and cross-cutting linkages at macro and micro levels to the overall economy

At the heart of the creative economy are the *creative industries*, defined as:

- the cycles of creation, production and distribution of goods and services that use creativity and intellectual capital as primary inputs
- a set of knowledge-based activities, focused on but not limited to the arts, potentially generating revenues from trade or intellectual property rights
- comprising tangible products and intangible intellectual or artistic services with creative content, economic value and market objectives
- constituting a new dynamic sector in world trade

The key figures who identified and defined the creative economy would broaden these definitions. John Howkins (creativeeconomy. com) published a major book in 2001 about the relation between creativity and economics.[4] Howkins considers 'neither creativity nor economics is new, but what is new is the nature and extent of the relationship between them and how they combine to create extraordinary value and wealth'.

To the 'creative industries' he would add a broader range of research and development in science and technology. When I interviewed him in London and asked about the importance of the creative economy he just answered: 'And what is actually left if you take creativity out of the economy?' Probably not that much! Today I, too, am convinced that applied creative thinking could reinvent a lot of the old economy in a post-recession world.

Richard Florida (creativeclass.com) has described an emerging social 'creative class' of professional, scientific and artistic workers who value individuality, meritocracy, diversity and openness, and whose presence generates economic, social and cultural dynamism, especially in urban areas, which he called 'creative cities'.[5] In these creative cities, argues Florida, members of the 'creative class' find 'the conditions they need to think, plan and act with imagination in harnessing opportunities.' His very broad definition of the creative class includes people in science and engineering, architecture and design, education, arts, music and entertainment as well as a larger group of creative professionals in medicine, finance and law, everyone in short whose economic function is to create new ideas, new technology or new content. He specifically mentions business-to-business creative services – design, advertising and entertainment – not only as *adding value* to every product but also as drivers of innovation for almost all industries. In this sense he argues that 'the economy is moving from a corporate-centred system to a people-driven one'.

I would take both Howkins' and Florida's arguments further and say that society and the economy in general need people with the capacity to think, plan and act creatively to solve problems, and

WELCOME TO THE CREATIVE ECONOMY, THE NEW GLOBAL REALITY!

'...neither creativity nor economics is new, but what is new is the nature and extent of the relationship between them and how they combine to create **extraordinary value and wealth**.' *(John Howkins)*

that the creativity of those who manage and run countries, cities and companies will determine future success in developing solutions – technological, conceptual and social – for our time's social problems.

Creativity, which once gave added value, is now mandatory in today's globally connected economy as vital to cultural, economical and social growth.

REFRAMING OUR IDEAS OF WORK

Last year I was talking to Dad about the changes around us and he came up with the notion of defining a new word for work, which would help change how people perceive the way they use their strength to earn money and build up a life for themselves and their families.

I loved his idea, though normally it is one I would expect from a branding specialist. If something doesn't work, then rename it and give it new significance!

But Dad is right. **Since the mid 1990s there has been a radical change in the organisation, meaning and language of work.** He has lived through this. Workplaces have been broken down into projects, most of them outsourced, with staff working on short-term contracts. From the days when most of us had a life-long job with an increasing salary and holidays there has been a shift to a more conceptual method of working, with people always visiting different places and social nets with less security and less consistency but more opportunity. These changes, taking place as knowledge-intensive economies develop, can mean a lot of opportunities if the *happiness* you want from life is not only dependent on job title, status and description.

Dad's main point was that the term 'work' is perceived negatively. Nowadays people get upset when they talk about their work, although they should be as proud of it as they are of their *vocation*. Instead people describe it with ambivalence. They are not really sure what to think about work: they talk about long hours, pressure, stress, dependence, fragility and insecurity. I personally know only a few people who really live their work as a vocation and talk about its productivity, fun, growth, meaning and vision.

After talking it through, we thought that the new word for work should express 'diversity, excitement, opportunity, personal growth and satisfaction'. Motivation, efficiency and productivity would be a logical consequence, but not ends in themselves.

If you have any ideas for how to substitute the word work and would like to share it then please email your suggestion to **newwordforwork@cpb-lab.com**. *Thank you.*

KEY COMPETENCES

In almost every developed country, two rates will constantly increase: the rate of those who are self-employed, by choice or circumstances, and the unemployment rate.

In the Europe we have now, at the beginning of 2013, some 25.9 million people – or 11.7 % of the active population – are unemployed.[6] The USA Department of Labor already estimated years ago that students can expect to have ten to fourteen different

WORK SHOULD EXPRESS DIVERSITY, EXCITEMENT, OPPORTUNITY, PERSONAL GROWTH AND SATISFACTION.

Motivation, efficiency and productivity would be the logical consequence, but not ends in themselves. Any ideas for a new word for work? newwordforwork@cpb-lab.com

jobs by the time they are thirty-eight years old. They didn't mean the same job in different companies, though: they meant different jobs with a different knowledge base.

According to their actual US Employment Projections 2008–2018 (bls.gov), service-providing industries – with business services and healthcare and social assistance to be expected to have the largest growth – are projected to add 14.6 million jobs.[7] That is 96% of the increase in total employment. (Business services include management, scientific, technical consulting and computer system design or everything that I would call service combined with creativity like computing, caring, catering, consulting, coaching.)

That growth in jobs is expected to be almost entirely offset by the decline in manufacturing jobs. What is more, and I'm sorry to tell you this – and with luck you will prove me wrong –you will most probably be sacked from your job one day. The interesting thing is that this will not *only* depend on your performance if you work in a larger company: many external factors will influence your professional career and, in consequence, your personal life. A few things are certain, though. We will have many more freelancers and entrepreneurs than ever before, and many people working to a contract rather than on full-time employment. Few people will have safe jobs and probably most of them will have government jobs.

I was interested to know what politicians recommended, so I travelled to Brussels to find out and had a long conversation with Jan Figel, European Commissioner for Education, Training and Culture from 2004 to 2009. He emphasised the taking of *life-long learning* seriously, the necessity of moving towards an entrepreneurial mindset which embraces human moral dimensions and employs horizontal and vertical skills. By that he means combining *sector-specific skills (horizontal)* with *self-skills (vertical)* such as thinking, communicating, teamwork etc. I thought Figel's reflections were so well tuned to reality that I now feel we should sometimes have a bit more respect for what they say in Brussels.

The recommendation of the European Parliament and Council for 'life-long learning' defines eight key forms of competence:[8]

1. Communication in your mother tongue
2. Communication in a foreign language
3. Mathematical competence and basic competence in science and technology
4. Digital competence
5. Learning to learn
6. Social and civic competence
7. Sense of initiative and entrepreneurship
8. Cultural awareness and expression

These forms of competence are interdependent and the emphasis in each is on critical thinking, creativity, initiative taking, problem solving, risk assessment, decision taking and constructive management of feelings. They will increase your *bargaining power* when you negotiate your work contracts and conditions. You will probably get a basic salary or fee with a performance bonus. So you may think you need to play a great game this week. Well, you need to play a great game every week and you need to play a good season in order to have any relevance within the market place. The rules are tougher, but with one advantage. **It actually will make people take a harder look at what they want and can do instead of following a standard career path.**

VISION: REINVENTING WORK AND LIFE

In the world we live in there is one key question: **what do you want to do with your one and only precious life?** Creativity and innovation are not strange habits any more. They are our new economy's backbone and we need to develop a vision to take that on board in our work and lives.

It is not a question of age, gender, nationality, continent or education. It's a question of ideas, knowledge, talent, attitude and the behavioural competences for a positive change. When everything is downsized people with these qualities will make a difference.

The deepest crisis since the Great Depression of 1929–39 gives us a unique opportunity to reinvent many areas of our lives to improve our society and lead change to a sustainable future. It also gives us the opportunity to reinvent ourselves as responsible global citizens.

We urgently need such change makers, creative visionaries and leaders, people with *substance:* real and valuable knowledge and expertise in at least one relevant area that increases effectiveness. We need people with the ability to synthesise information and combine creativity with business strategy. We need creative leaders with *style:* an understanding of aesthetics and the power of design and design thinking. **We need creative leaders with *conviction:* ethics, integrity and beliefs and an idea of how a better world could be.** We need people with *grace:* the ability to listen and talk to diverse people, to understand and act within new business realities and sometimes just say 'thank you'.

This is the new mindset we need: an informed, active, responsible and relevant citizen in our global society.

The individual may be his or her own company. A personal brand, self-responsible and self-managed, in search of continuous training and lifelong learning, can help in all markets, with skills that are constantly adjusted and updated in response to on-going structural labour market changes. There are no limits any more. This is great if you have the right skills, the right knowledge and the right attitude to seize this opportunity. If you don't, however, the scenario is much more complicated. The people left in traditional businesses and companies, including yours, will be given many more responsibilities. This is great. But these people will also be aware that they have more competitors waiting at the door to replace them for a lower salary. Reality shows consistently that the strategies most companies use to react to any change that is triggered by new technology means more pressure for the individual to create value.

Don't get me wrong. I am not saying these are easy-to-solve problems and there is a simple prescription for recovery. What I am saying is that we have to start at one point, and that some day is today, which is infinitely preferable to tomorrow. And that if each of us is optimising and taking responsibility for our lives, small but positive decisions of many individuals will have a big and positive impact on our future society. This is *bottom-up thinking*.

The approach is simple, yet very effective. We need people who challenge the status quo, create their futures and lead their lives to help others. There is a huge demand on people with the emotional and intellectual capacity to relate and react to a complex world in a state of constant flux. We need people who combine *substance and style, conviction and grace.*

THE CREATIVE ECONOMY NEEDS CREATIVE LEADERSHIP: PEOPLE WITH SUBSTANCE AND STYLE, CONVICTION AND GRACE.

We need people who challenge the status quo, create their futures and lead their lives to help others.

03
_CREATE!

How To Create Opportunities

HOW TO CREATE OPPORTUNITIES

Remember yourself as a kid? Think about the role-playing you did, think about all the things you created. Get those drawings and models out! If you have serious problems recalling these experiences and you do have not children yet, then go to the nearest nursery school and just watch kids at play. As you watch them remember the old adage: 'If children gave up the first time they fell, they would never learn to walk.' What you will see are little human beings playing, laughing, enjoying different roles, imagining different professions. But those children will steadily decrease their play and fun. As they get older, they will be told that this kind of behaviour is not logical and therefore not correct.

One of the leading authorities in the field of creative thinking, Edward de Bono, defines three ages of life. The age 0–5 is the age of *'why'*, 6–11 of *'why not'*, and 11–75+ of *'because'*. Our business culture is biased towards logic and rational thinking. Our educational system is often reduced to a *'one right-answer'* system. De Bono claims that 'since Aristotle, Socrates and Plato 2,500 years ago we believe in logic and argument to prove theories either right or wrong, trying to find the ultimate truth and putting things in boxes.'[1] This seems to be true as we have myriad *left-brainers* who believe in pure analytical faith: people, especially politicians and managers, who are pushed to use the numerical, rational and logical part in the left hemisphere of the brain. And look where we have ended up. **Sameness wherever you go.**

When I asked Ferran Adrià, the groundbreaking Catalan chef at the El Bulli restaurant in Roses, Spain, how he would define creativity, his answer was simple but clear.

'**Creativity is not copying,**' a maxim he learned from French chef Jacques Maximin. Yet copycat seems to be a strategy nowadays. It is like playing rock-paper-scissors with beginners. They usually choose rock and also tend to copy the winner. It is predictable. And it is about exploiting, not creating. Ruthless exploitation, remember, is the opposite of sustainability. In the creative economy *sustainability* means the care and sustainable renewal – that is, environmentally, socially and financially sustainable – for our resources.

CREATIVE THINKING: A KILLER APPLICATION

No simple definition of 'creativity' can explain all its dimensions. People often talk about artistic, scientific and economic creativity, but, as I see it, each one of those is part of something wider. Creativity is a culture, a philosophy, a point of view about the world and its future. Knowledge is important. Imagination is as important as knowledge. The key, however, is to combine knowledge, imagination, business, intelligence and pleasure with creativity. This kind of creative thinking is the killer application. The result? The capacity to identify real problems and create new solutions, opportunities, categories and markets.

Artistic creativity is traditionally seen as an altruistic way of generating ideas and ways of interpreting the world without necessarily aiming to produce value. Scientific creativity is more often about curiosity and experimentation in a very narrow field. If we talk about business creativity we normally mean the process of new product development. I would focus instead on *creative thinking*

CREATIVE THINKING IS A KILLER APPLICATION!

The result? The capacity to identify real problems and create new solutions, opportunities, categories and markets.

as a constructive, participative and highly productive thinking team process, one that is multidisciplinary and is a combination of business thinking and creativity, knowledge and imagination. It can be applied in very varied areas to:

a) identifying the *right* problem
b) developing, designing and applying tangible and/or intangible solutions that have economical value *and* are still environmentally, financially and socially sustainable.

Why does creative thinking yield such good results? Because its diverse and multidisciplinary approach gives us the possibility to see things from different points of views right from the beginning and therefore a higher chance to come up with new and relevant solutions. Creative thinking brings solutions. Creative thinking translates into productivity. The first step of the process, however, is to identify and understand the problem. Maria Grazia Mazzocchi, founder and former CEO of the Domus Academy in Milan (domusacademy.com) described it to me in this way: 'It is very, very important, before you pick up a pencil, to open your mind and ask yourself what the true needs are of the society we are working for.'

Many a time we come up with solutions that don't respond to a problem that is correctly identified. Or, even worse, we aren't aware that we have a problem. As Bertrand Russell, the British philosopher, put it, 'The greatest challenge to any thinker is stating the problem in a way that will allow a solution.' It is therefore crucial to apply creative thinking to problems. This is as true today for companies as it is, more than ever before, for people.

Nowadays we need to be conscious of the consequences

THE QUALITY OF OUR CREATIVE THINKING WILL POSITIVELY INFLUENCE THE QUALITY OF OUR LIFE!

To use both sides of the brain, its logic and magic, is the new requirement to reshape our work and life.

of our solutions, how they affect our environment, our economy and our society … and society as a whole. Again I would quote Maria Grazia Mazzocchi: 'sustainable design is the true, intelligent and clean design we need.' That is why we need creative leadership, which helps us to understand 'where to go', 'how to get there' and 'with whom'. It also creates platforms for creative thinking: for building up ideas, motivation, inspiration and, most importantly, participation. This is the opposite of our traditional approach to analytical thinking, which is more concerned with judging and finding errors. This shift will affect your work and life, positively influencing the way you create, play, learn, communicate and differentiate.

Such creative thinking starts with your creativity. Now please don't tell me you are not creative. Of course, you are right. There will always be people with a greater aptitude for creative thinking, but that doesn't mean everyone else is totally incapable of coming up with new solutions. **Creativity is a skill, just as thinking is.** Just as you can train your memory you can also train your creativity. Many non-creative people generate excellent ideas by using different techniques. The jump is from divergent-idea generation in a spontaneous manner to convergent-idea generation in a structured manner – thinking. As Edward de Bono (edwdebono. com) has written: 'Creativity can be learnt by anyone by using systematic *lateral thinking* techniques'. Lateral thinking is about reasoning, which is not obvious at first sight and does not result from traditional sequential logic. De Bono also argues that the single factor which helps to determine any individual's creativity is their perception of themselves as 'creative'. The same is true of thinking. Confidence fuels the person's ability to be creative and think creatively.

THE KEY
IS TO COMBINE
BUSINESS
AND CREATIVITY.

3

Knowledge and imagination, intelligence and pleasure.

HYBRID BRAINWORK: LOGIC AND MAGIC

Everything starts with our minds. Neuroscientists' insights have changed the way we think about our brain. Decades ago people thought that by the age of seven their brain had fully grown and that little growth would be possible after this age. Today we know that until the last day of your life your brain can generate between 500 and 1,000 new neurons a day: not that much if you think the human brain contains about 50 to 200 billion neurons in all.[2] What this means is that your brain can grow if you feed it and adapt to change if you want to. Personal growth is indeed possible. In other words, you can teach an old dog new tricks!

Besides that, we now know that the right side of our brain is responsible for interpersonal understanding.[3] The left hemisphere of your brain recognises what is said, the right hemisphere how it is said. The left hemisphere is where language is based, the chief faculty that differentiates us from animals. It is the right part, however, that gets the tonality. This skill makes human beings more sophisticated communicators. People using the right side of the brain are the empathetic ones, the ones who read between the lines, the ones who synthesise instead of purely analysing. They are the ones who understand relationships within relationships. Or who simply see the bigger picture. In a more complex world in which we encounter diverse cultural mindsets and need to communicate and interpret more subtly than ever before, to understand situations and to take decisions, the right side of the brain is invaluable. **One requirement to reshape our work and life is to use both parts of the brain, its logic and magic.**

So we need people who understand the capacity to use the

left (logical) and the right (emotional) side of the brain. Thanks to the left side of our brain we have increased life expectation and standards enormously. Today we need to practise creative thinking, which is built on new approaches, new ideas that will help us to come up with new solutions – a balance between left and right brain thinking. Can you imagine yin without yang, Holmes without Watson, James Bond without Q? This balance also helps to eliminate the fear of failure and encourages participation. It is much more social and can maximize output. It is a more practical approach to resolve problems or issues and improve future business results.

Funnily enough, we all use both parts of the brain, but sometimes quite unconsciously. If you really want something important from your husband, wife, friend, colleague or your parents you spend quite a long time thinking about the right words, tone and moment to ask your question in order to minimise the chance of your request being rejected. Children are incredibly adept at this if they want something from their parents. They know exactly how and when to talk to their mum or their dad to get their wishes fulfilled. Again just head for the nearest playground and watch. We all have the capacity to cultivate this skill.

All those who only trust in logic need to reconsider at this stage. Most of the time we do not behave logically. How many times have you convinced someone by using only logical arguments? How many times have you been at a meeting at which the solution was obvious and logical to you, but wasn't accepted by the participants? Why? Because it didn't inspire, people didn't feel it, maybe they didn't feel you, and so they refused. Winston Churchill once said: 'Before you can inspire with emotion, you must be swamped with it yourself. Before you can move their tears, your own must flow. To convince them, you must yourself believe.' Some of the younger ones of us fall in love up to three times a day. This is not logical, yet very emotional and great. And that is OK, it is why we come up with great things. Most great things in life are not logical. The great Italian film maker, Federico Fellini, once said that only visionaries are true realists.

That's why I often tell students we men should leave our collars and ties at home. They seem to me to be the visible metaphor of a separation between head and heart – a separation which allows you to do business logically, with the head, without being affected by our emotions.[4] Now we know that we need both, however. Emotion and imagination work together well in creative thinking. I talked to designer Tokujin Yoshioka (tokujin.com) in Tokyo about this. His view is that good design is not about arranging shapes and things, but 'designing people's emotions and feelings'. We have so many problems to solve, but there is a positive side to that. Ideas make the difference and are what really matters. **We live in a perfect time for launching great ideas, new solutions and new concepts.**

Only one thing holds back our creativity: we fear failure and rejection. What we need to understand, however, is that failure and rejection are part of the creative culture. Howard Schultz, the founder of Starbucks (starbucks.com), had to do more than 250 presentations to raise the early-stage funding to start his coffee-bar chain. Innovation demands failure. Everyone who has achieved much has suffered setbacks and rejections. The interesting thing is that nowadays no one really cares about it. Something new can't be expected to be perfect. We need to understand that without those

MOST GREAT THINGS IN LIFE ARE NOT LOGICAL!

---

*How many times have you convinced someone **by using only logical arguments**?*

fools who try the impossible we would still be living in the Dark Ages. So have respect for those who take risks. Challenge concepts, challenge yourself, find your personal benchmark.

CREATIVE LEADERSHIP IN DEVELOPMENT

Sports companies such as adidas, Nike or North Face understand this search for creative excellence. Their mottos are *'impossible is nothing'*, or *'just do it'* or *'never stop exploring'*.

'Think Different' was a slogan for Apple created by advertising agency TBWA/Chiat Day in 1997. Apple, as always, was ahead of its time. The 1997 commercial showed people like Albert Einstein, Martin Luther King, John Lennon, Muhammad Ali, Maria Callas, Martha Graham, Jim Henson (with Kermit the Frog), Frank Lloyd Wright etc. – people who thought differently and who believed in a different future, in ideas and abilities. Today those personalities could be Kofi Annan, Steve Jobs, Bill Drayton, Konstantin Grcic, Bono, Ferran Adrià, Tokujin Yoshioka, Zaha Hadid, Marc Gobé, Miuccia Prada, Muhammad Yunus, David Lachapelle, Nelson Mandela, Quentin Tarantino, Rem Koolhaas, Sir Ken Robinson, etc.

This *'Think Different'* campaign is more relevant than ever today, in times of instability and insecurity when the enthusiasm to dare and to risk is missing. When it was created it was dedicated to 'the crazy ones, the rebels and the misfits', 'the ones who see things differently', characterised as the ones 'who are not fond of rules and do not have respect for the status quo'. The ones people may disagree, but also the ones you cannot ignore because they 'changed things' and 'they push the human race forward', 'because the people

ONLY ONE THING HOLDS US BACK: WE FEAR FAILURE AND REJECTION.

What we need to understand, however, is that failure and rejection are part of the creative culture.

who are crazy enough to think that they can change the world, are the ones who do'. That line is part of the commercial's copy. You can still see it on YouTube (youtube.com).[5] And I strongly recommend it to you. **We urgently need that mindset, and we need people with the confidence to take advantage of creativity and imagination to change things for good – not only for themselves, also for society.**

This kind of thinking has to be cultivated, however. In today's world it's not enough to get a twenty-five-year educational overdose of facts, figures and methods to manage your career successfully until you drop. My feelings about this were confirmed when I talked to Amanda Spring, partner of the creative recruitment company Pakter (pakter.com) about my experience as a qualified graphic designer with an MBA. These are two different disciplines that did not seem to work together ten to fifteen years ago. She said that nowadays 'the people who have the standard educational profiles are struggling. It's the people with a special background who were previously sometimes misunderstood and under-appreciated, who are sought out for *hybrid roles.*' A general manager, for example, might now be recruited precisely because he or she studied architecture or fashion at some point.

In our educational system so much still depends on the ability to reason logically from cause to effect. But effects are the result of many causes. The world today is much more complex than before. Lots of people are good at describing the past and managing the present, but creative thinkers, often called rebels and misfits, are great at describing how the world would look like by asking: *what if?*

This way of thinking challenges education in general and, more specifically, executive education. It implies that MBAs (Masters of Business Administration) are not the only 'high potentials' any more. If we reflect on the evolution of crucial skills to lead a consumer goods company we detect the following: first there were engineers, who either invented or at least really understood the company's product; then there were lawyers, as the contractual dimensions became more complex; now there are MBAs, or Mfins (Masters of Finance) able to understand balance sheets, income statements and profit and loss, as today's companies require constant justification of financial activities. This is very important but it means managing the status quo. As future success depends on finding solutions and creating opportunities, we need a new hybrid creative leadership mindset. The difference from MBA thinking? Instead of authority there is *inspiration*, instead of hierarchy there is *collaboration*, instead of delegation there is *participation*. The obsession with avoiding mistakes becomes an obsession with innovation and how to learn from mistakes.

I am not talking here about making business or finance people creative nor of turning creative thinkers into business people. I am talking about making savvy business people understand and respect creative thinking. Making them learn about and accept new ways of thinking, new ways of communicating, new ways of seeing the world – and, along the way, new ideas, new markets and new opportunities. Wouldn't that be great? On top of that, creativity has ideas – our thoughts – as primary raw material, which has no side effects.

It is also important to emphasise that design-aware people and other creative thinkers need to understand much more about business methods and tools to analyse and understand industries, markets and companies, to speak the language of business, to take on board its responsibilities and the peculiar pressure of quarterly

WE NEED
A NEW HYBRID
CREATIVE LEADERSHIP
MINDSET.

*Instead of authority we need **inspiration**, instead of hierarchy we need **collaboration**, instead of delegation we need **participation**.*

results. Hence many great ideas and solutions fail because of insufficient business knowledge. I talked about this problem in Munich with industrial designer Konstantin Grcic (konstantin-grcic.com). His point of view left a lasting impression on me. 'There is no contradiction between the creative and business side of this work. They are related, and I think I have to understand the business side of it to be creative in the right way. I have to understand all the mechanics of the market, of the industry, of calculations, of costs, of taking risks and investments.' Business and design schools have now begun to create collaborations to educate and form this new profile leader.[6]

Helping creative and business people to respect each other, understand and benefit from each others' way of thinking can nurture a generation of creative entrepreneurs who implement their vision via inspirational and motivational thinking, collaboration and communication in order to develop new and sustainable business models. For a company this can mean success, for the individual freedom, growth or simply fulfilment.

One good example of this is *social entrepreneurship*[7]. Why are many social enterprises non profit-making and, as a result, highly dependent on donations and support? Wouldn't it be much more interesting to have a social enterprise which earns serious money? Isn't that a vision? Value creation in being socially responsible? Change the world, make some money, make more changes and so on ...

For examples U2's Bono's *Product Red* is a straightforward business idea to transform collective consumer power to help others, specifically people infected by HIV in Africa, where 60% of all people with AIDS die. How does it work? You, as a consumer, can choose to buy any of the (RED) Products, from Apple's iPod to Converse Chucks, from Nike's red laces to Armani sunglasses at no extra cost. The company which makes the product gives up to 50%

of its profit to buy and distribute medicine to help AIDS sufferers in Africa. The impact? Go to their website joinred.com and you will get the actual result. I think this is a valuable idea for today's brands to raise awareness and offer consumers the possibility of giving sustainable help to solve serious problems. The notion is based on the thinking of Bill Drayton, founder of Ashoka (ashoka.org), a global organisation that identifies and invests in leading social entrepreneurs). 'The world is different because you are different.' And that starts with thinking differently!

CULTIVATING CREATIVE THINKING

Creativity cannot be forced, but it can be fuelled. Even politics seems to have taken on board its economic importance.

When Jan Figel, the European Commissioner of Education and Culture, initiated the *European Year of Creativity and Innovation* back in *2009*, he declared that its aims were: 'to raise awareness of the importance of creativity and innovation for personal, social and economic development; to disseminate good practices; to stimulate education and research, and to promote policy debate on related issues.'[8] The key message, targeted at young people, educators, firms and policy makers, as well as the general public, was that 'creativity and innovation contribute to economic prosperity as well as to social and individual wellbeing.' I think this is also a sign of change and a great initiative, and I hope it is not only a one-shot campaign.

This doesn't count only for the developed world, however. According to the United Nations the creative economy offers opportunities to companies in developing markets to leapfrog into emerging high-growth areas of the world economy. No doubt they will take this chance. And don't think that the rise of Chinese and Indian competitors means low-cost and low-quality imitations flooding the world markets. Leading companies in these countries are now competing on innovation in telecommunications, biotechnology and green energy solutions. Wasn't innovation supposed to be the competitive advantage for European and American companies? Anyway, it is a wake-up call for everyone to cultivate creative thinking and define new strategies for innovation.

If one thinks about cultivating creativity, one can also think about the steps we need to take to allow that to happen.

1. CREATIVE THINKING IS VERY SOCIAL

In both artistic as well as business creativity you can have a great idea by yourself. Creativity, however, especially in a business context, needs interaction with other people. The application of an idea will in most cases require collaboration and interaction – not just with anyone but with the right people. For this you will need people with the same way of thinking as you – with the same cleverness, imagination and especially motivation – but who have different roles and backgrounds to make the conversation rich and the application successful. Ideas exist to be discussed and debated, especially in small groups. It doesn't make sense to sit alone at home and run around in circles. You need people with whom you can exchange your ideas, who show you a different point of view and who are willing to collaborate and sum up.

2. CREATIVE THINKING NEEDS THE RIGHT SPACE

The right environment favours creativity. It needs to feed your soul. You alone can decide where it is. Think for example about your home office, the place where you feel comfortable, together with your books, your favourite chair, your music and enough space to put and move your Post-it notes full of your ideas. Great companies offer creative spaces so people feel comfortable. People sometimes travel or move to creative cities such as London, Shanghai, Amsterdam, Buenos Aires, and so on, in search of what Richard Florida describes in his book *Cities and the Creative Class* as a place where you can find 'good air, connections, research capacity, venture capital investment and clusters of producers' to nurture the creative class and its members.

3. CREATIVE THINKING NEEDS TIME

Many people share Calvin's (from cartoon characters Calvin and Hobbes) belief when he says: 'You can't just turn on creativity. You have to be in the right mood. What mood is that? Last-minute panic!' Certain pressures and last-minute panic may sometimes help, but finding 'solutions needs time …' Creativity doesn't work from 9 to 5. Ideas come and go and you need time to sit down and reflect. Time alone. Time to play around. Time to experiment. Time to read. Time to think. Time to converse with others. An idea is something organic, it has to grow, and that implies that you need to invest time. Google, for example, encourages creativity: their people spend up to 20% of their time on a project of their choice.

4. CREATIVE THINKING NEEDS DIVERSITY

Many companies still retain the strange habit of choosing candidates with similar profiles for their jobs, and the same happens with business and design schools. So what do you expect from the same group of people? The same answers. Diversity is the mother of creativity, however. **See diversity as an opportunity.** Multiculturalism is the answer and not the problem. My experience is that culturally diverse teams, if well managed, have the highest potential to create and innovate, while having a much higher *learning curve* and, incidentally, more fun.

5. CREATIVE THINKING NEEDS VERSATILE RESOURCES

Observation, research and visualisation are important skills. It is important to collect articles, advertisements, pictures, objects, movies, music, bits and pieces of daily life. Read different newspapers and design magazines. They may be from New York, Barcelona, Buenos Aires or Tokyo. Are you familiar with *The Senken* (senken-intl.com), Japan's most widely read fashion daily? Alternatively, visit a museum, of history or design, whatever you please. Become a design detective – visit shops all over the world. This will be the material that will enable you to create a *mood board*. A mood board is the visual illustration tool used either to represent the atmosphere or the feel of an idea. It helps to inspire you and your team, and to create momentum.

DIVERSITY IS THE MOTHER OF CREATIVITY.

See diversity as an opportunity. Multicultural societies are the answer and not the problem.

6. CREATIVE THINKING HAS THREE STEPS

This is the key process and the basic value chain for developing ideas. First in your mind, then on paper or digitally, and finally in reality. You need the ability to project, to visualise and to evaluate. How do you evaluate? Well, put three different products on your table. How do they affect each of your five senses? Positively or negatively? Ask yourself why. Define criteria, remember the objective and keep always the consumer in mind. Evaluate.

7. CREATIVE THINKING MEANS LOTS OF IDEAS

An idea is not a singular thing. It's about having a lot of them. First quantity, than quality, trying to filter out to reach the right one. Write those ideas on Post-it notes and stick them on your walls. If an idea stays in your head for more than a few weeks, then there is something about it. Follow your instinct.

8. CREATIVE THINKING NEEDS STIMULUS

Stimulus may come from many sources: other art forms, conversation, research, reading, experience. Remember, frustration can be inspiration too. How many times have you already been frustrated about products or services? Instead of blaming the provider, why not do better yourself? Channel your annoyance. Try to improve a product you don't like, make a sketch and send it to the manufacturer.

9. CREATIVE THINKING NEEDS PROTECTION

Most creative people work as *creative entrepreneurs*[9], being their own boss, mostly because they love freedom. As the one who is living off creative ideas with economic value, however, you need to understand how these creative products can be protected by copyright, designs, trademarks or patents. A great way to learn more about *Intellectual Property*[10] is given by the European Union on handsoffmydesign.com. The IP handbook explains the most common types of Intellectual Property you will come across as a designer, what your rights are and where and how to protect them.

10. CREATIVE VALUE-CHAINS NEED TO BE ANALYSED

One of the key methods to analyse a creative business model is value-chain analysis.[11] It helps to understand the total chain of adding value to your idea, product or service. From (a) creation and the initial idea to (b) production and reproduction to (c) marketing and distribution until the stage where the client (d) consumes your product, this will help you to understand what you or others need to do. For example, to develop a movie is probably the most complex value chain you can have in terms of time, cost and collaboration on all four stages of the value chain. It starts with the script writer, then the production company, then comes the director, the marketing and distribution of the movie to cinema, TV, DVD and so on. It is much easier when you, as a graphic designer, develop a corporate identity for a start-up and you work directly with the owner or if you sell your photographs via your own website straight to your clients, without resorting to any intermediary.

IDEAS: PASSION TO PRODUCTION

Speaking from personal experience gleaned over the last twenty years, I would say that 49% of all great ideas do not come to life purely because of their creators' laziness (good at thinking but not doing) and a further 50% because of other people's resistance (boycott of ideas). The conclusion is that not more than 1 % of all great ideas survive.

The key here is that the communication of your creative thinking needs to be motivating, getting people to act in support of, and understanding, your idea. First you need to motivate yourself, then others. Rather than simply satisfying others intellectually, you need to inspire them. I have gained one personal insight from working with ideas and people over the last twenty years: 'If everyone loves your idea, get nervous, something is bound to go really wrong (or is fundamentally wrong), for sure. On the other hand, if you encounter a lot of resistance, there is something to your idea.' Conflict during discussions and highly involved emotional personal reactions are good signs you are on the right track. Take care, though: there is always someone in every team who will want to kill your idea.

What, then, is a good business idea? It is a smart solution to something people have a need for, no more and no less. A good business idea is a simple one. In the end just one thing decides whether or not a business idea is successful and that is the market. At the *point of sale* people will decide if your idea is worth buying, or not – if your idea created a simple and accessible solution to a specific problem or not.

CREATIVITY NEEDS TO BE CREATED THREE TIMES.

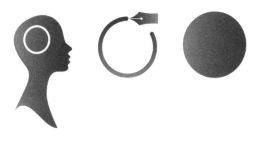

*First in your **mind**, then on **paper** or digitally, and finally in reality.*

Here, more or less, is how the cycle of idea development works. One day you detect some needs. You gain a valuable insight. Sometimes it's just because you are hit by a really bad product, or bad service, or even because you cannot find a solution for a specific problem. Then you think, how, surprisingly, there seems to be a gap in the market here. Someone else, surely, must have come up with your idea already? You may stop at this point or you can go further. You now have an idea in your head, though. If you want to take this a stage further you can put it down on paper, design the product or service, find out who can and will help you, and calculate costs. Then you produce a small amount of your product or service and you test it 'live' in the market place.

Ideas need design and aesthetic visualisation. Interestingly enough, most people have problems differentiating between creativity, innovation and design. They use those words in any context, but many times wrongly. Creativity is the mental process of developing ideas. Innovation is the way you apply ideas. Design is the form or style you give the idea. Finally, design has officially been rewarded by most people's recognition that it is part of their life – it is not an opinion leader. Nowadays it is seen as something that enhances your life. People know, understand and talk about designers, new designs and the possibility of expressing the spirit of their life through design, be it in their apartments, their workplaces, their clothes or their travel destinations. Well-designed innovations are economically crucial for many companies and can give a sustainable competitive advantage. To work in design is also personally rewarding and emotionally engaging. **Design can improve people's way of life, work and thinking.** It is not style over substance, however; that was how things were in the past. Now it is substance and style. The combination is vital and, therefore, the key to the future.

What kills good business ideas? I mentioned before that creativity is very social. Collaboration with other people is central to innovation. Collaboration and teamwork may also become an obstacle, however. Most of us have good ideas about the future *but* leading the creative process, its realisation and implementation are a big problem. Collaboration, day-to-day working, knowing who is doing what, when and how, being aware of each person's role within a team, guaranteeing constant and fluid communication, accepting decisions taken by the group against your personal opinion and still supporting each other, all with a sense of commitment and responsibility, are true challenges.

IDEAS GROW FROM INSIGHTS

There are two approaches to developing ideas. The simplest is to come up with an idea then try to find a market for it. In this case you need to create demand. But remember: creating demand is always complicated and cost-intensive.

Satisfying existing demand is a much easier and more feasible process. The starting point to achieve this is to have a full understanding of markets, tendencies and trends, targets and their specific needs. Coming up with creative ideas to satisfy demand is about empathy, understanding people and identifying their problems. To do this you will need to be highly disciplined, able to structure and analyse. You will also need to research and investigate thoroughly. **Our world is full of problems which need urgent solutions.** From AIDS, cancer, climate change, diabetes, drugs, hurricanes, human trafficking, oil spill and obesity to poverty and terrorism, to name just a few.[12]

You then need to be able to detect tendencies. Remember in the first chapter I asked you to analyse three tendencies relevant to your reality? Think about them. To give you a few more examples: microproducts (products getting smaller), micromobility (urban transport), healthcare (ageing society), eco-everything, life-long learning, etc. Or consider designing new services, a discipline known as *service design*[13]. Remember the global trend towards service and its power to revitalise existing products and categories. Don't you think there is a need to design services at airports, say, in hospitals or in government administration?

How many hours have you spent 'waiting' in your life? Is it fair to say that you wait for at least half an hour every time you go to the doctor? And from that arises another question: what can we do to avoid waiting? First you research a specific target market, most probably the one you are closest to, for insights, then you develop ideas which could solve the problem.

For example, assuming that the majority of patients have mobile phones today, why do I always have to wait in my doctor's waiting room? Wouldn't it be great to be informed via text or, even better, a cost-free email to your smartphone, so you, as a patient, can use your time more constructively than in waiting? I know it means investment, time and money for the health service or doctor, but wouldn't that be a useful service which would respect people's time? Another example can be found in the airline industry. Why are airlines still not capable of informing you right away when they have lost your luggage? Why do you have to wait first for ages at baggage retrieval, then talk to someone at the information desk who has no idea what has happened, and finally negotiate with someone at a call centre until you are told what is going on?

CREATIVITY
IS THE MENTAL PROCESS
OF DEVELOPING IDEAS.

INNOVATION
IS THE WAY YOU APPLY
IDEAS.

DESIGN
IS THE FORM OR STYLE
YOU GIVE THE IDEA.

The airline knows exactly where your luggage is, even before the moment it fails to make it on board the plane, and they do have your email address and your mobile phone number, as you need to leave an exhausting amount of information about yourself when you buy your ticket online. Wouldn't it be great to be told of the problem when you get off the plane, with a well-worded apology until they give you further instructions as to how and to get your luggage back? That's the consumer-centric, empathetic approach to develop and design new services that make life easier. And it will be rewarded by their customers.

Companies that are successful understand one thing: research is the transformation of money into knowledge, and innovation is the transformation of knowledge into money. Clear? Great.

Incidentally, sometimes strategies end with insight instead of innovation, which may be interesting, but is not necessarily of value. **An insight is a clear, deep and sometimes sudden understanding of a complex problem or situation.** It is more like a good question. An insight in a business context, for example, is detecting that people do not enter fashion retailers Zara or H&M straight away – they go there at the end of their shopping expedition. First they get inspiration from their favourite shop, but perhaps these are pricey boutiques or brands, then they go to the larger, cheaper retail stores.

Translating that insight into ideas is innovation. Zara and H&M could assume that their customers, mainly women, arrive exhausted, sometimes nervous, after hours of shopping with little time left. They could offer a healthy energy drink, for example, a massage or secure storage facilities where the shoppers can leave their bags while they complete their purchases unhindered. Innovation is the conclusion of the journey towards a discovery of people's aspirations. This connects ideas with what motivates consumers. To be innovative in retail you need to be a permanent mystery shopper.

As you work on developing ideas you will also find there is always someone who wants to kill your idea, or at least tries to demotivate you, so it is important to prepare yourself for that. Actually you will always face three sorts of people who put up resistance to your idea:

1. The person who is by nature against everything. (The motivation behind this reaction is often fear.)
2. The person who doesn't see and understand the goal or objective, and therefore is not motivated. (This is a lack of understanding or a major communication problem.)
3. The person who has the same idea as you but is too weak and not sufficiently brave to develop it and to put it into action. (This is about envy, which is the most dangerous of all feelings.)

Within the process of developing business ideas, there will always be someone who wants to test the concept by proposing market research. Don't get me wrong. I am a huge supporter of market research because it gives you the possibility to gain neutral and in-depth insights at the beginning of an innovation process. *Ethnographic research[14]*, for example, can really take you a big step ahead. My experience makes me believe that while market research is important, however, it should never be a substitute for your intuition. Please trust your intuition and your experience and fight for your idea. Do you think that Lady Gaga would have survived any focus group?

RESEARCH IS THE TRANSFORMATION OF MONEY INTO KNOWLEDGE.

Innovation is the transformation of knowledge into money.

One problem here is that people tend to give politically correct answers when they know they are being observed. Almost everyone answers 'yes' when asked if they clean their teeth three times a day. It's equally easy to say you would potentially buy a product, but something different happens if you are asked to get the money out and buy it now. My recommendation is, therefore, to use market research in order to understand your category and gain insights, but once you have an idea take it straight to a test-market in which you will see in reality if people like your product or service and whether they will pay for it.

I have focused here on creative thinking as a thought process to generate new ideas and solutions that have business value. By creative thinking I mean a process of building up ideas while deferring judgement on them, in order to eliminate fear of failure and increase motivation to participate in this process. In such a process we need a hybrid mindset to bridge the distances between heart and head, right and left brain hemisphere, passion and production. Our best ideas are based on intuition and insights, emotions and feelings. It's a question of combining *pleasure and intelligence,* a way of thinking which has to be cultivated at all kinds of schools and universities as well as in companies. But the best thing about it is, you have everything you need to succeed – your brain and your heart! That's all it takes.

Assignment — 2:
CREATE AND/OR IDENTIFY
YOUR BEST BUSINESS IDEA

You, as a creative person, understand diverse cultures. You feel empathy and sympathy for others. Think about the people you get along with well. What interests do you share? Are you a connoisseur, a real expert in any subject? In which markets? Where do you have first-hand experience? Are you a member of a club? Are you reading a special interest magazine? Do you find yourself identifying people's problems in any areas where you can come up with a new idea, service or product? Can you improve an existing product?

My personal suggestion Your own experience is fundamental. Try to fill a demand you see exists. It is much easier. Try to come up with a lot of ideas, then focus on one, or take the possibility of working with one idea which has been on your mind for quite some time and which you thought you would never have time to think about properly. Here we go.

1 — Think:

a) Which interests do you share with other people? Where do you have first-hand experience and insights?

_____

_____

_____

_____

_____

b) In which areas are you able to identify people's problems and can you come up with a new business idea, service or product?

_____

_____

_____

_____

_____

c) Can you improve an existing service or product?

_____

_____

_____

_____

2 — What is your best business idea?

Which is the best idea among the ones you always think about, but never had time for?

04
_GROW!

How To Grow Personally

HOW TO GROW PERSONALLY

We need to find meaning in what we are doing. That means finding a match between your personality and the job you do – and that means knowing your own personality. It is interesting to see how many *Generation Y[1]* students are adding sense and meaning to money as a work priority. They saw their parents working with complete loyalty and conviction, without question or criticism, risking their health, losing spouses, children and friends slowly over thirty-five years, only to find themselves sacked one grey Monday morning without any reasonable explanation.

So those young adults don't share the same vision of their working life as their parents. Long years of effort in exchange for salary rises and slow promotions up the career ladder seem pointless to them. Generation Y wants to make things happen fast – as fast as they can search for information on Google – working independently, internationally and focusing on things that matter personally to them. Often that is translated into cool and interesting projects that range from spending a winter as a ski instructor to doing an internship with a favourite designer in London, or being a curator in a gallery, working as a social community manager or developing an ethical fashion brand.

This vision of life is just as important to *Generation X[2]*, members of which were born in a manual age and later acquired digital skills – yes, that's me! In a few years from now *'the war for talent'[3]* will be a reality for everyone, even for the older *baby boomers[4]* – that is, people who were born in the years following the Second World War.

'For them', and for other generations, too, everything – work and life included – is becoming more complex. The requirement for

WE NEED TO FIND MEANING IN WHAT WE ARE DOING!

That means finding a **match between your personality and the job you do** — and that means knowing your own personality.

dealing with this complexity is the same for every generation: **know yourself and match your personality with your job.**

STRATEGY AND PERSONALITY

Who are you? Good question, no? The study of personality can be interpreted as the study of masks people wear. The word 'personality' is derived from the Latin word *persona*, which was used for the mask worn by actors in ancient Rome to change their appearance. Nowadays, however, personality generally refers to our attempts to capture an individual's 'essence': the assets we have, the complex set of qualities and attributes (behavioural, temperamental, emotional and mental) that characterise us as individuals and make us unique and distinct.

No two people are the same, not even twins. What, then, is our personality built around? Personal experiences, beliefs, expectations, desires, values, and behaviour, mostly based on our interaction between culture and the individual – meaning society and us. An individual's personality also shapes the behaviour and technique that underlies problem solving. Your personality is your starting point. It is where you begin your journey towards a new vision by creating and leading positive change through personal growth. This is why we need to understand our personality, and have a primary focus on personal development to handle this new and sometimes contradictory world.

Now, with the conclusions and insights you have gained about creative thinking, comes the assessment of your personality.

How do you define your individual human capital, your substance, your competences and skills, knowledge and creativity, personal attributes such as courage and drive, empathy and integrity, in everything you perform and produce? Your strategy springs out of your personality. Not everyone can do every job, but assessments help us to define roles you can play and maybe even unearth a hidden talent in an unsatisfactory job. Bear in mind that when you feel good you do your work best. A study by Proteus, a London-based consulting company, states that only 9% of European workers have a job that fits their personality structure.[5] So what are the other 91% doing? **Could this be the reason, perhaps, why so many of us have that strange feeling of not fulfilling our total potential?**

Knowing your own personality helps you also to understand your learning style, which is important. Today you need to take life-long learning seriously. And it is also a great way to learn about yourself, and your relation to your peers.

CREATIVE PERSONAL BRANDING: WHAT IS IT?

Of course there are many ways of talking about personality. Here I am going to focus on four criteria underlying the idea of personality as a starting point for creative personal branding.

These four criteria are **substance, style, conviction and grace**. Growing out of an experience-based learning model, this approach to personality can generate value-based entrepreneurs, change makers and creative leaders. Their personal growth is based on insight into themselves and the world around them: the way we communicate, give and receive effective feedback, identify and handle conflict, understand the dynamics of culturally diverse groups and leadership style. Here you will detect your **substance:** your expertise on a specific topic, your education, knowledge, experience and references. It is good to have a broad background and to know many things, but you have to be an expert in one area. I am thinking of Danish physicist Nils Bohr's definition of an expert as a person who has made all the mistakes that can be made in a very narrow field. So now you can decide what is missing for you to be an expert. You can also detect your **style:** the way you talk, listen, write, perform and dress. And your sense of **conviction:** your perspective on ethics and integrity, your moral principles and firmly held beliefs or opinions based on your values. It is also about your aspirations and your questions. What do you live for? How you can add value to a positive social change? Finally there is social **grace**, which I see as elegance in your relationship with society. Sometimes that means simple things like saying 'hello', 'goodbye', 'please' and 'thank you'. Sometimes it means more profound and challenging ways of interacting with society, which can involve considerable sacrifice.

I can almost hear some of you say: 'But I don't know who I really am, what I am good at and what I really want in life. So how can I know my substance or style?'

No problem. You are not the only one, believe me. In my work with many diverse and creative cultures and mentalities, in workplaces as well at schools, I have always found three types of people besides the few for whom everything is clear and who know exactly where to go:

STRATEGY SPRINGS OUT OF YOUR PERSONALITY!

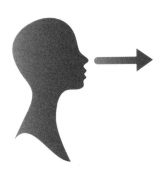

Not everyone can do every job, but assessments help us to define roles we can play.

1. Those who don't know where to go. They never really thought about it.
2. Those who know where to go, but only because someone told them. They don't understand why.
3. Those who know where to go, but not with whom. Remember, you cannot do everything by yourself.

No matter how old you are, what level of experience you have or what position you are in, you should start to find out who you are. The benefits are worth the effort of thinking, reflecting on and refining your goals, vision and mission as well as the strategy you will need to get there. This is a complex task. It was never an easy one, either emotionally or intellectually, and it has been made harder by the pressures on all of us today. Listening to my Grandpa or my Dad – who belongs to the baby boomer generation – is like listening to *Jurassic Park* when it comes to their professional advice. This is not disrespectful, it simply is not real for us. We, primarily members of Generation X, and you, members of Generation Y (digital from day one – that's probably you), now choose where to live, study, work and die. That is a real generation gap. We have total choice, but nothing left to rely on when it comes to work. With so many choices comes this strange feeling of making the wrong decisions. That puts a lot of pressure on the individual and, inevitably, affects your personality.

My own emotional reaction to these changes, when I listen to my Grandpa or Dad falls somewere between envy and anger. As I reflect on the current situation with them, I feel like an *agent provocateur*. For knowing ourselves is made harder one the one hand by an environment that is confused by possibilities, opportunities

CREATIVE PERSONAL BRANDING:

substance,

your expertise on a specific topic, your education, knowledge, experience and references.

style,

the way you talk, listen, write, perform and dress.

conviction,

your perspective on ethics and integrity, your moral principles and firmly held beliefs or opinions based on your values.

and grace.

the elegance in your relationship with society.

and freedom, and on the other hand by pressures, demands and competition in an ever changing environment.

HOW TO IDENTIFY YOUR OWN HUMAN CAPITAL

The aim here is to discover your potential through your personality. If you have no time for these assignments, just read, think and put down the most relevant keywords or draw up a mental map at each point.

If you have trouble answering a question, please don't get bogged down by too much analysis. Go to the next point and come back to the question once you have more time. It's a challenge, but you will see that it is one of the greatest journeys – yours. I am not saying these are easy questions. What I am saying is that it is worth reflecting upon those questions. The working life for our generation (and the following one too, for certain) will be extremely long, so it makes sense to invest a couple of hours, an entire day, or even longer, to think about these questions and find answers to them. I know that many of you have been thinking about them, some of you for years, but few with any tangible result. Why? Well, you probably did it by yourself, thinking in circles. We sometimes do not see the wood for the trees. Our personality structure is too complex to answer such questions on our own, however. The perception we have about ourselves differs from the one other people have of us, especially with the things we are good at.

An example? Some people have the talent to talk in public

TO IDENTIFY YOUR HUMAN CAPITAL IS A CHALLENGE, BUT YOU WILL SEE THAT IT IS ONE OF THE GREATEST JOURNEYS – YOURS!

One hint: very often your weaknesses are the flip side of your strength.

and are admired by others for that. Instead of taking advantage of this strength they are permanently trying to optimise other weaknesses. Mostly because that was the way we were taught in school. They are not aware of the many people with stage fright they could help if they could only master their natural talent and learn how to put it across. The same is true of people who are very skilled at writing, translating, creating, selling, negotiating and so on. Instead of gaining recognition, growing personally, feeling good (remember how good it feels when someone says, honestly, 'thank you, you did a great job'?) and, incidentally, earning money, they focus on doing the same thing and staying in the same frustrating situation.

One last hint: very often your weaknesses are the flip side of your strength.

Assignment — 3:
DETECT AND UNDERSTAND YOUR OWN MOTIVATION

Life is about drive. You have to find the elements that trigger you and your personal interests. Think about what you have to offer to the world, things that motivate you. My personal drive, for example, is to see people grow. Detect personal aptitudes which create fun, motivate you and help others. What was your first successful achievement in your youth? Once you have answers to those questions you will be able to define your objectives, vision, mission and values. In the end you want to have an answer to the following key four questions.

- What drives and motivates you?
- What are the things you are really good at?
- How does that help and add value to others?
- What three experiences made you glad, sad or even mad?

My personal suggestion If you have no time to do this exercise, just read, think and put down the most relevant key words or draw up a mental map at each point. Bear in the mind the Pareto principle, named after Italian economist Vilfredo Pareto, which states that roughly 80% of output comes from 20% of input.[6]

1 — Drive:

First you need to find out what motivates you. Is it money, fame, interesting projects, friends, travelling, being creative?

a) What drives and motivates you?

_____

_____

_____

_____

_____

b) What are the things you are really good at?

_____

_____

_____

_____

c) How does that help and add value to others?

_____

_____

_____

_____

_____

d) What three experiences made you glad, sad or even mad?

_____

_____

_____

_____

Now think about the following points:

2 — *Your history:*

Think about your heritage-inventory. The aim is to track down and understand your history. That means to reflect on where you are from and how that impacts on your individual human capital, your competences, knowledge and attributes.

a) Think about your birthplace and the year you were born.

b) Think about your family – each member of your family – their education, characteristics, beliefs and professions.

Write a quick summary.

3 — Structure your life up to now

What has brought you to this point? Think about how your life has developed. The younger among you will find out that the first part of life is about success, the older that the second part of life is more about meaning.

a) Identify the most important milestones in your life. Break them up into seven-year stages (0–7, 7–14, 14–21, etc.). Write a short summary of each stage.

4 — *What are the things you are good at?*

How do you see yourself? Think about your characteristics. How would you describe yourself in each of the following areas:

a) General skills: music, sports, maths, languages, etc.

b) Specific skills: technological, creative thinking and economical skills, etc.

_____

_____

_____

_____

_____

c) Expertise: your substance, the areas in which you really can measure yourself against others.

_____

_____

_____

_____

d) Personality: funny, extroverted, intuitive, sensible, hunger for knowledge, laid back, etc.

_____

_____

_____

_____

e) Physique: tall, slim, colour of eyes, etc.

_____

_____

_____

_____

_____

f) Needs: sleep, favourite foods, clothes, etc.

_____

_____

_____

_____

g) Interests: reading, travel, dance, painting, etc.

_____

_____

_____

_____

5 — How would you identify your main influences?

Think about the impulses and inspiration that influenced your life.

a) Think about conversations, books, people, films, games, speeches, art, travels or other key experiences – things or people that gave you impulse and inspired you to act.

Write these down in whatever form you like: notes, a mental map, a drawing, a computer spreadsheet etc.

6 — *Think about and define your personal values*

Values are fundamental, they are part of your personality, and you need to be aware of them. Your value system is a set of rules you follow to make the right decisions in life. Things you strongly believe in and guide your life such as excellence, honesty, creativity etc. This is your modus operandi.

My personal suggestion
Expect surprises in part b) of this exercise.

a) Define the five values which are most important to you.

_____

_____

_____

_____

_____

b) Check those values against those of your friends or the company you are working for.

_____

_____

_____

_____

Great, you have thought now about who you are and where you're from. You've defined what drives you. Before the next step or assignment, I would like to introduce two concepts.

PEER PRESSURE AND THE INNER RING

CREATIVE PERSONAL BRANDING—GROW

'The Inner Ring' was the title of the memorial lecture at King's College, University of London, given in 1944 by C.S. Lewis, Professor of Medieval and Renaissance English at Cambridge University and, by the way, a close friend of J.R.R. Tolkien, author of *The Lord of the Rings*. Lewis used the concept to describe one of the most basic desires which drives us as human beings, the desire to belong. Many of us are not really satisfied with who we are and constantly compete with other people, trying to impress them and be part of an invisible ring of people. Most of us are unaware of this inner ring. But this need to gain respect is a never ending response to *peer pressure*[7]. Once you are finally part of an inner ring another one will crop up.

If you depend on other people's opinions when you take a decision it will sap your energy substantially if they don't agree. It will mean that when you take high-impact life decisions, you will consider what your inner ring will think about it and keep in your mind your natural desire to be part of that ring. It is what Tolstoy calls the *'unwritten system'* in *War and Peace*. It is the dominant desire to be inside and part of the ring and the terror of being left outside.

'The people in your inner ring' are most probably not really interested in you, they may even see you as a competitor and will not help you honestly. The people I would like you to consult for feedback are seriously and honestly interested in your personal growth. That is quite a different thing. You may say: 'Oh my God, no, I don't want to, I'm embarrassed to ask people about myself.' Feedback is really important, however, and is probably one of the most effective tools you can use. **Feedback makes champions.**

WE SOMETIMES FEEL WE ARE AT A PERMANENT OLYMPICS, PARTICIPATING IN ALL DISCIPLINES WITH GLOBAL COMPETITION.

A strategy to cope with it? Find out what drives you!

So now, having thought about your inner ring, it is time to do a cross-check and ask people for feedback about your strength and weaknesses.

COACHING: INVEST IN YOURSELF

Assuming we have a permanent World Cup going on around us, it's interesting to see that athletes and other sports players have coaches – but usually we don't.

For an athlete a coach is someone who asks the right questions, gives feedback, helps to define strategy, focuses on the athlete's strength, improves preparation and defines the right time to recover after peak performances. We lack such inspirational coaches and experienced mentors to give us the feedback that will help us to make choices in the rest of our lives. I believe *coaching*[8] can and should start at universities. I had a coach on my MBA course. The coaching offer was actually decisive in me taking the Master's degree at that college, but in my case the coach was not fully prepared and lacked experience or interest. It was very demotivating and I was on the verge of abandoning the MBA course because of it. A year later, when I decided to live and work in Barcelona, I tried another coach to help me work on this transition, and ever since I have been convinced of the power of coaching. It takes years of experience and many different tools to accompany other people successfully on their way. Now, years later, as I coach my own students, individuals and teams, I understand the complexity of the task. This is made greater by the fact that most prospective students do not really know what to expect first time around.

My own coaching philosophy is that of the Creative Personal Branding programme (CPB). The method is based on the idea that the individual, who was never completely free, is imprisoned in our limitless world in search of excellence. As individuals, we are always observing and evaluating, and are always on our own when it comes to taking decisions. The risk of failure is enormous and therefore inhibits playful exploration. To master these challenges we need new skills. The creative personal branding programme is designed to offer individuals an exciting way to understand challenges today, and to develop opportunities based on personal growth through self-insights. The programme may therefore help individuals of all walks of life move on to create vision for their work and life.

At the core of the programme lies each individual's personality. In sessions, working as diverse intercultural teams or on a one-to-one basis, we reflect, interact and react to new challenges. Radical changes are not desired or desirable. The system, and we ourselves, are too fragile. Instead we look for ways of finding balance and wellbeing within ourselves and between teams, and of reaching objectives and responsibilities. We have to play with the contradictions of modern work and life. CPB means transition. **CPB means reinvention.** In such an atmosphere solutions to the challenges will arise surprisingly, but meaningfully, in the right atmosphere.

Now that I have been working with this method for years and seeing its results, I am more than ever convinced that coaching is one of the best investments you can make in yourself. Coaching is a great tool for institutions, companies and the individual as a way of differentiating themselves and improving the efficiency of their performance.

Everyone who has finished a marathon knows the experience. For the average person there is no chance to succeed unless you are well prepared. Even that is no guarantee of success. Everything is much easier if you have the right people supporting you, however, working on your aptitude, and helping you to keep up your attitude. Your working life is like a marathon morphing into a decathlon. It is therefore not a question of being fast at the beginning. It is a question of reaching the finishing line, even though exhausted, and still having a smile on your face. A coach can help you to achieve this.

Assignment — 4:
LOOK FOR FEEDBACK

The main question behind this is: how do people perceive you? The problem is that few people give us honest feedback. But – sorry, Ken Blanchard (kenblanchard.com), but I need to borrow your line here – feedback is the real breakfast of champions. It lets you know how you are doing, it reinforces changes and increases self-confidence.

My personal suggestion The big problem with feedback is who, when and how to ask. Parents are spiritually many times too removed from their children (and normally never change the perception they have of their child), and most professors or work colleagues are not really good at it. Often they have had not chance to learn or they just don't care. Most people are not trained to give valuable, honest and constructive feedback. Universities emphasise presentation skills, but how many students or professionals are trained in giving valuable feedback? Most of the time it is a game of 'tell me something nice about me and I will tell you something nice about you.' Mutual admiration helps nobody, though. Neither does point-scoring by those who want to put you down as a way of dealing with their own insecurities. What is more, the higher up the ladder you move, the less the possibility of receiving honest and constructive feedback. Feedback is so important, however, that you need to use every possibility to get it from the right people. Make sure you have defined your goals; the more specific the better.

1 — Get feedback on yourself

Ask people you respect – people who have the possibility to observe you and who you have identified as seriously interested in your development – to describe your strengths and weaknesses, your behaviour in specific situations.

a) Define the people you will ask for feedback.

----

b) Ask them kindly to write their feedback down. Explain to them you do not want them to judge you, but to describe precisely how they see you.

c) Now encourage judgement where you are looking for it. Ask them what they find special and unique about you. Ask them what they think is your greatest and clearest strength, and also what are your greatest weaknesses. Ask them to give you professional advice. Do it now.

2 — Respond to feedback

a) At the end please say thank you. You are using other people's goodwill.

b) Keep their notes and letters for the rest of your life.

c) Take these notes out and read them once in a while, especially before making important decisions.

The more people you ask, the more you can optimise your action. The most difficult thing is to start asking for feedback, but the more experience you acquire, the better at it you will be.

'Excellent', you have survived the assignment. Well done! And, how was it? Not that bad? Isn't it good to know what people you respect think about you, and to get confirmation that you are not so bad in their eyes?

You have now a starting point to learn more about who you are, where you are from, what drives you, what you love to do and what principles you value – and you now know your strength and weaknesses.

DON'T BE DRAGGED BACK!

Time and money are two principal reasons mentioned for not taking certain key steps. On the other hand there are factors which can drag you in the wrong direction.

1. CONFIDENCE IS CRUCIAL

Last summer I was talking to a friend of mine in my hometown and we reflected that ten years ago we didn't know anyone unemployed. Later there were a few unemployed people, but since there were job offers around they were socially seen as losers, not capable of finding jobs. Now we know many people without work: people with a good education, valuable work experience and at their best age. Are these all losers then? I don't think so. I honestly believe someone can't be that 'good' one day and then that 'bad' the next. Losing your job or not finding work, an experience which many people undergo nowadays, will affect you and won't do anything to increase your self-confidence. There are people aged around thirty to fifty who have already been sacked two to three times over the last five years. I even know of one case where a person got sacked three times in six months – a new record up to now. I haven't heard of anything similar before. The loss of confidence that goes with such experiences is the last thing any of us need, as most of us already have a lot of doubts and are very self-critical. It is said that if we talked to other people as our inner voice criticises us, we wouldn't have any friends at all. **So, please remember, attitude is as important as aptitude.**

2. AGAIN YOUR BRAIN

Your brain is your real home office, on the go *24/7*. It is your real sustainable competitive advantage. It is the inter-disciplinary, multi-tasking think tank which can help you answer the basic question of 'who you are' and 'what you should do next'. This will help you discover your potential and define your strategy, your vision and mission. Most importantly, it will help you to implement it. Always bear in mind: for successful people there is only a fine line between plan and action. Remember, too, you need to use the left hemisphere of the brain, the logical side, and the right one, the intuitive side, together. Both hemispheres need to work smoothly together like the Omega Moon Watch[9], because then, if you are trying to reach for the stars, you will be well prepared.

3. REDUCE YOUR NEGATIVE STRESS

On my holiday I went to my old tennis club to play at 9 am on a regular working day. The courts were full of people around forty-five to fifty years old playing doubles. I was surprised to see people who never had time ten years ago because they were workaholics. Talking to them they told me that they had been sacked or were diplomatically given early retirement. A change of concept forced by drastic changes of the environment. It sounds great to have a lot of time off, more time to spend with your family and friends. Well, sure, but only if you have the necessary financial resources to do so. Even then, that enforced leisure doesn't make you happy. This is a contradiction of our times: you either have a job and money, but no time, or you have no job and no money but loads of time.

The fact is, we all need work, we need to add value to

society, we need to have that feeling of being part of something greater. How many of us are unhappy with the situation we are in, and not doing what we would really like to do? Or, even worse, not doing the things we are really good at? Frustration and resignation are just a question of time. We can't get rid of the feeling that we have much more potential than we apply. We need stress, but only positive stress.

Yes, there are two forms of stress: positive and negative. There is a huge difference between them. Positive stress, also called *eustress*, increases performance, makes you excited about a new, challenging and demanding situation, which you think you can handle. It gives you energy and is essential to bring zest to life. Excitement is what it is all about, and makes life worthwhile. Insufficient positive stress is followed by boredom, hopelessness and apathy. Negative stress, called *distress*, can cause physical and mental damage. When too much negative stress is present individuals feel frustrated, fearful or angry. Have you ever seen people three years after retirement when they don't have any hobbies? Remember Grandpa Simpson from *The Simpsons*? That's how they look. Just because they lost their rhythm, it is slow death by boredom. The same happens to people who have lost their jobs. They have time but they cannot enjoy it. Losing work seems to be normal these days. Headlines in the *Financial Times* and other business newspapers are full of it. Friends and family tell me of such cases right across the market and in every category of job. Change is tremendous, a serious virus, slow but lethal for many individuals, and with severe consequences for their families. I also see many people leaving their workplace because they don't fit in and others who haven't had the good fortune to get sacked and become slowly ill because of their work.

It is important to distance yourself from negative distress and create positive stress in your life.

4. KNOW THE LINE BETWEEN KAIZEN AND KAROSHI

In this wild market environment it is increasingly difficult to position and differentiate yourself from your many competitors. So there is a new game to be played. Do you have a game plan? No? Game over. So you need to have a plan, more specifically Plan A and Plan B.

If you have doubts concerning plans, let me explain two things to you. First, planning is essential because it gives you the possibility to manage deviations. Second, it is not a plan to increase your working hours. You have probably thought about this but let me tell you, in case you are having some doubts, it is not sustainable to start working sixteen hours a day. I know, because I tried it. It is not healthy, physically or mentally. You will not increase your performance. Time is against you: the curve will go down, faster and lower than you ever thought possible. In some countries the rate of burnout is already higher than the rate of heart attacks. If you reach the eighty-hour working week, than you are probably close to 'death by overwork'. In Japan, sudden death from a heart attack or stroke brought on by overwork is known as *karoshi*. This first emerged as a major problem in the 1970s, coinciding with cuts in jobs and a resulting increase in individuals' workloads. Many Japanese employees were therefore working an average of twelve hours a day.

So take care in the current deregulated labour market, which seems to justify overworking and underpaying large sections of the workforce. Nobody will deny that hard work is the base of success. But there is a fine line between *kaizen*[10], the Japanese term for continuous improvement, and *karoshi*, death by overwork. Prepare yourself constantly. **Opportunity always favours the prepared mind.**

EXCITEMENT IS WHAT IT IS ALL ABOUT!

*It makes **life** worthwhile.*

But to slave, save and retire is really not a great concept. Instead it makes a lot of sense to spend some time thinking about what's coming next. I am talking about you and your future. As Woody Allen says: 'I think a lot about the future, because this is the place where I will spend the rest of my life.' You need to work prudently, passionately and with a lot of power.

ETHICS AND VALUES AS A MODUS OPERANDI

Leaders may have many tools and skills, but the wrong conviction, ethics, values, motivation and especially attitude. Still too many CEOs look like Tintin, behave like Quentin Tarantino's version of Lucky Luke, take decisions like they are in a cowboy film and do business with the Daltons to enjoy immense and unjustified bonuses. But a 'show me the money' attitude is not a sustainable leadership style for a company leader, and less so for someone who leads people. Quite a few people who I have interviewed in the course of my work have told me they think this is the real origin of the current crisis. Crisis in leadership means personal crisis. This is quite simple. If someone goes over the top, someone else will pay for it, and normally the weaker one. This is our status quo. Such an attitude can drag a whole workforce in the wrong direction.

I have come to the conclusion that we have more a crisis of leadership than any other thing. You could also call it a crisis of business ethics and integrity. Rudi Plettinx, Vice President and Managing Director of the Center for Creative Leadership (ccl.org), told me during an interview last year that he would also describe

SLAVE, SAVE AND RETIRE IS NOT A GOOD STRATEGY.

*Instead it makes a lot of sense to spend some time thinking about **what's coming next**.*

the current finance and economic crisis as one of leadership. He describes creative leadership as the way to think beyond and expand personal boundaries to be effective, but he assumes that the educational system is not yet preparing people for the challenges of the future. I also talked to a Buddhist monk about the same subject. He reflected on the crisis as a spiritual one: 'If your mind is less jealous, less competitive and with less anger, your mind is brighter.'

Still, too many companies and bosses believe economic value is the only *raison d'être* – the reason to exist – for a company and salary the only motivation for individuals to work. This is not true. There are, however, changes and new approaches to leadership. The Thunderbird Business School (thunderbird.edu) for example, one of the top business schools worldwide, now formally defines an *oath of honour*[11], believed to be the first of its kind at a business school. Since 2006 they have formally included it in the overall educational experience, application to study there, curriculum and at graduation where students are actually are asked to sign up to the Thunderbird Oath of Honor. It reads:

'As a Thunderbird and a global citizen, I promise I will strive to act with honesty and integrity, I will respect the rights and dignity of all people, I will strive to create sustainable prosperity worldwide, I will oppose all forms of corruption and exploitation, and I will take responsibility for my actions. As I hold true to these principles, it is my hope that I may enjoy an honorable reputation and peace of conscience. This pledge I make freely and upon my honor.'

It sounds very nice and will, with luck, make an impact because there are many new ways of making business and profits which bring about positive social change. These new ways of doing business will recognise social and environmental problems and use entrepreneurial principles to create and manage societal change. Remember, though, corporate social responsibility[12] (CSR) starts with individual social responsibility (ISR). CSR will be decisive not only for traditional business success, but also for future social acceptance. To combine creative with social leadership will bring exceptional new leaders. In this new area of responsibility we need more women in leadership positions who have the natural capacity to lead, listen and observe, and use their expertise and substance to encourage and start dialogues without prejudice and with transparency. Leaders need to be able to communicate their values and visions without imposing them. Making substantial improvement is the aim. As Kofi Annan, former secretary-general of the United Nations once said: 'There will be no important social change without females.' Imagine a company which aims to create positive social change through its business. Combining business principles with social ventures in this way has enormous power, enormous synergies and benefits. Just think about the work of Muhammad Yunus, the founder and manager of Grameen Bank, (grameen-info.org), a microcredit banking system for the poor which supports social initiatives like housing for the poor, micro-enterprise loans, education loans and scholarships etc. Incidentally, 97% of the lenders are women, and the bank has the same percentage as loan recovery rate. A quick way to review these kind of businesses is the *Fast Company Magazine* (fastcompany.com), which annually publishes a list of the twenty-five best social entrepreneurs, which the magazine defines as organisations 'using the disciplines of the corporate world to tackle daunting social problems.'

CORPORATE SOCIAL RESPONSIBILITY STARTS WITH INDIVIDUAL SOCIAL RESPONSIBILITY!

*Leaders need to be able to communicate their ethical values and visions **without imposing them.***

VISION AND MISSION: WHERE TO GO AND WHY

I am convinced it is very hard to score without a goal. I am also convinced it is very difficult to perform well and efficiently if you don't know your vision. Or, even worse, if you have a vision but you don't live up to it. That is as true for the individual as for companies. How many companies, departments and individuals have a great vision and mission statement on their website, but the only thing they really want is to increase revenue? Poor vision because that doesn't connect with peoples' drive and motivations. With poor vision you normally achieve the opposite effect and you end up in the poor dog corner of the *Boston Consulting Group Matrix*[13] (BCG Growth-Share Matrix), the corner where you find products with low share of a low growth market. It's just a question of time.

A proper vision, and living up to it, are both absolutely necessary. A vision tells you what you want to become. It gives you an idea of where you want to be in the future. Once you have defined it, then it is much easier to answer what your next step is. You will know how to make it. Because you are then able to transmit it and you will also find out who will come with you on the way. Best of all, you will know when you have arrived at where you wanted to be. This is important: many people define entry strategies, but not exit strategies. Having a vision is like having a dream: a perception, a feeling of how we would like to have things around us.

The late fashion designer Alexander McQueen (alexandermcqueen.com), for example, had the vision of a 'lasting luxury brand to be here 150 years'. Linkedin's Vision (Linkedin.com) is 'to provide economic opportunity to every professional in the

WHAT IS REALLY IMPORTANT TO YOU? YOUR VALUES DEFINE YOUR MODUS OPERANDI!

Do we have economic crises or a lack of ethical leadership?

world'. Ashoka (ashoka.org), the organisation for social entrepreneurship, 'envisions an Everyone A Changemaker™ world. A world that responds quickly and effectively to social challenges, and where each individual has the freedom, confidence and society's support to address any social problem and drive change'. At PUMA (vision. puma.com/us/en), for instance, they believe that their position as the creative leader in Sportlifestyle gives them the opportunity and the responsibility to contribute to a better world. A better world in their vision – PUMAVision – would be safer, more peaceful, and more creative. Strategy is a plan to get there. Strategy is foremost about how to use your strength to take advantage of the opportunities in an ever-changing environment. Puma breaks their vision down to programs such as *safe.puma.com* (focusing on environmental and social issues), *peace.puma.com* (supporting global peace) and *creative.puma.com* (supporting artists and creative organisations). A strategy should help you to be in a better position tomorrow than you are in today. Visions are growing and maturing – they are not unique acts though they should always be realistic and work in daily business.

I always suggest three approaches to define a vision. All three should be visual. The aim is to be balanced. You need to find balance between yourself, performance, relationships and sense or meaning. There are many industries which make a good living by giving support to unbalanced people. To be balanced is important, otherwise even a small crisis will have a huge negative impact. It is interesting that the ancient Greeks only gave people about fifty years old the possibility to be politicians. Why? Well, these people had already successfully survived the most important crises in their life.

HAVING A VISION IS LIKE HAVING A DREAM:

a perception, a feeling of how we would like to have things around us.

Assignment—5:
WRITE UP YOUR VISION AND MISSION STATEMENT

1 — *Vision*

Again I would ask for your input. Try to do this as quickly as possible. Think, but then act and write down spontaneously. Don't lose track. Remember the assignments you did in the first chapter and the chapter on creativity: the three tendencies you defined for the next fifteen years, the opportunities and threats you detected and your best idea.

My personal suggestion Put everything together and define your vision, mission and goals. Go one step further: think about your vision and mission.

a) Define a wish list of what you want to achieve in the most important areas of your life. Not just your professional ones. The professional wish list is very important, but it has to be in line with all the other really important areas of your life: personal, health, career, friends, family, finance, recreation and spiritual. Respecting the needs of your loved ones, your financial situation, the desire to travel or engage in sports, your intellectual and emotional wishes, and so on.

b) Your billboard.

If you have trouble writing and defining this in words, collect pictures of things you feel attracted to. I know people who have pictures of their dream house, the cities they want to visit, objects they want to buy, etc. It is great to update this frequently.

c) Your obituary notice.

Imagine yourself looking back at your life. Ask yourself what you want to be remembered for and what you want to have achieved by then. Focus only on the most important points.

2 — Mission Statement

You know the question: what is your mission in life? But do you know your answer?

A mission statement defines what a country or an organisation is all about. To give you examples: Ashoka (ashoka.org) strives 'to shape a global, entrepreneurial, competitive citizen sector; one that allows social entrepreneurs to thrive and enables the world's citizens to think and act as change makers.' Linkedin's (linkedin.com) mission is to 'connect the world's professionals to make them more productive and successful.' But it also counts for people, for you. In Muhammad Ali's (ali.com) words: 'All I did was stand up for what I believed.'

My personal suggestion This phrase needs to offer orientation and motivation to help control and evaluate your actions. A good mission statement is personal, positive, written in the present, visualised and emotional. One reminder. According to the Austrian psychotherapist Victor Frankl (viktorfrankl.org), author of *Man's Search for Meaning*: 'We don't have to invent mission and meaning of life, it's already in us, we just have to detect and identify it.'

a) Write out your personal constitution. The idea is to express value and vision in one phrase. A mission statement answers three key questions. What do you do? For whom do you do it? What is the benefit?

Well done! You made it. You have detected your potential, got a much clearer picture about where you are from, what your likes and dislikes, strengths and weaknesses and your values are. Together with the three tendencies, the opportunities and your best idea, you have defined where you want to be in the future (your vision) and what you need do to get there (your mission).

GOALS: IT'S HARD TO SCORE WITHOUT A GOAL

I know what you are thinking – goals are such a pain! On the one hand this is true, and you will certainly have much more fun without bothering about goals pressurising your free-thinking mind. Let me remind you of something mentioned earlier, however. It really is hard to score without a goal. Goals have to be realistic, motivational and inspirational. You need to make them specific, measurable and time-bound. Before you start to define them, make sure that you understand the difference between goals and objectives. Goals are the desired outcome we seek, bringing us towards our vision. Objectives are specific and concrete outcomes and milestones towards our goals. First you set your goals, then your objectives. Don't get me wrong, objectives are also goals, but figure further down the hierarchy.

We need goals, not for a rush or kick, but because creating sustainable goals is essential. We need goals that are worth suffering for and investing your passion, your time and your money in. We need to do the right things (effectiveness) instead of just doing things right (efficiency). How many people went up the career ladder quickly only to find out that the ladder is propped up against the wrong wall? The right goals can give great satisfaction if they are related to adding value or to helping other people. For most people time is the most important tool, but instead of a watch to control time, it is probably better for us to take a compass. That helps us to ask ourselves the right question: where do we want to be/go/work tomorrow? The slowest, the one who is focusing on his goals, will always be faster than the one who is running around without a goal.

IT'S
HARD TO SCORE
WITHOUT A
GOAL!

Goals have to be realistic, motivational and inspirational.

Let me give you one example to make all of this clearer. My goal is to inspire other people to find their way. My objectives are to write two books about this topic and run at least five workshops this year. You see the difference? The goal is more abstract, the objectives translate it into measured steps. These would be difficult to work out without fixing on the goal.

Assignment — 6:
DEFINE YOUR GOALS AND OBJECTIVES

Pure action without goal definition is your biggest enemy. Once you define and focus on a particular goal, however, related things seem to be everywhere. This is selective awareness. It is the same as when you want to buy a red Ducati (ducati.com) and, strangely enough, you see more red Ducatis around than ever before. The same happens with opportunities: if you define them you will see them. If not, how can you see, detect and identify them?

My personal suggestion A goal has to be measurable, feasible and very motivational. Think of *Alice in Wonderland*, when Alice asks the cat: 'which way should I take?' And the cat asks: 'Alice, where do you want to go?' Alice says: 'I don't know', and the cat answers: 'Well, then it doesn't matter where you go.' The key benefit is that once you have defined your goals in the most important areas of your life, you can invest time, energy and money.

1 — *Goals*

Try to write down first your three most important goals, and then your five most important objectives for year one, two and three (starting with this year).

Goal 1

_____

_____

_____

_____

Goal 2

_____

_____

_____

_____

Goal 3

_____

_____

_____

_____

2 — *Objectives*

Year 1 (5 objectives)

_____

_____

_____

_____

Year 2 (5 objectives)

_____

_____

_____

_____

Year 3 (5 objectives)

_____

_____

_____

_____

That's it! Congratulations.

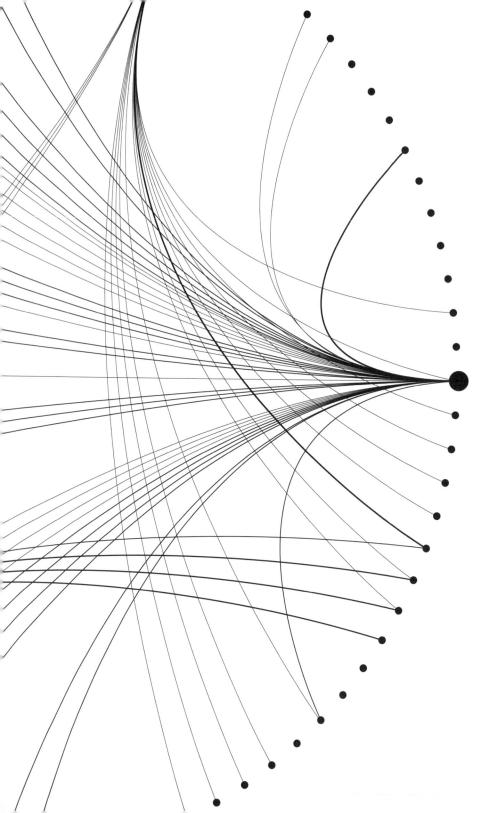

05
_DIFFERENTIATE!

How To Differentiate

HOW TO DIFFERENTIATE

You now know how to identify or create opportunities, you've analysed your assets, you've detected market needs and thought about the most important elements in your professional field for the next decade. You've also looked at your own personality, defined your vision, mission and your values. Now we are going to look at how you differentiate yourself from others. That might also be called branding.

A lot of people think a brand is a product, but it isn't. Branding means neither awareness nor is it a concrete 'thing'. It is more of a metaphor for complex phenomena, a story, a meaning, an identity. Remember what I mentioned about the 'essence' of personality? Exactly. It is about your assets, a complex set of qualities and attributes – behavioural, temperamental, emotional and mental – that characterise you as an individual and make you unique and distinct from others. **This is what defines a brand: its personality.** It is also what differentiates a brand from a non-brand. Isn't it interesting how close those two concepts are? Brand personality and the personality of an individual?

Think of Barack Obama, one of the world's most high-profile personal brands. 'Yes, we can' was a great slogan – simple, straightforward, easy to understand. It meant motivation and action, a point of view which confirmed the possibility that we can change an existing situation. It had a similar power to Nike's 'Just do it', a slogan which turned millions of couch potatoes into runners. Obama also understood the high impact of new technology, the art of communication and the power of perception. Pictures of him using his Blackberry made him the role model of an updated, technologically driven and more sophisticated generation of politicians. It made him somehow 'accessible', even though only five people have his phone number. With the help of his electoral e-campaign he connected with the masses, especially people from the younger generation, via social networks and platforms. He offered to collaborate, was proactive and used interactive media to transmit his message. This way he gained twice as much in donations as his electoral rival John McCain in 2008. He had 20 million viewers watching his speeches on YouTube compared to the two million of his competitors. And he made 3.5 million friends in social networks compared to the 850,000 of McCain. You could say Obama managed to leave a sustainable interactive brand footprint. His twenty-something advisors found a way to deliver the right branding message to the right people in the most effective way[1] and in 2012 they followed on through leverage of social networks. Demographics suggest he carried voters in the 18-34 age range by taking his message to those discussing issues. When it came to Twitter and RSS feeds his team came up with twice the content of Mitt Romney's team.

BRANDING: HOW TO LEVERAGE A BUSINESS IDEA

Many people love brands while other hate them, thinking it's about overselling. Our fascination with the words 'brand' and 'branding' is amazing, though. Both professionals and people on the street talk about 'brands' in all kinds of contexts. Almost everything you

ALMOST EVERYTHING YOU CHOOSE IS NOW BRANDED.

*From **products** to **services**, cities to countries, sports figures to politicians.*

choose is now branded, from products to services, cities to countries, sports figures to politicians. And this is even truer in the age of connectivity, when social networks give not only companies but also the individual a low-cost and highly efficient opportunity to showcase strength, skills and experience, to map out and build up our private and professional human relations. One thing is sure: love or hate branding, it is definitely one of the most efficient strategies ever to leverage[2] a business idea in highly competitive markets. It is no secret that branding has long been the most efficient method to find new professional opportunities in an unstable work environment, with all-out competition pressurising the individual. That has only increased with branding's new online dimension. Witness first of all these long established brand ideas:

- Swatch (swatch.com) ... Swiss watches. A disposable fashion item of which you can buy more than one.
- Victoria's Secret (victoriassecret.com) ... and its angels. Seductive underwear.
- Paul Smith (paulsmith.co.uk) ... colourful and sophisticated. British Fashion Design.
- Smart (smart.com) ... for sophisticated urban needs. A micromobility car solution.
- Zaha Hadid (zaha-hadid.com) ... futuristic and questioning. Bespoke architecture.
- Brompton (brompton.co.uk) ... personal transport. Folding bike.
- Kingdom of Bhutan (grossnationalhappiness.com) ... a Tibetan country. Rethinking political values with GNH (Gross National Happiness) instead of GNP (Gross National Product).

YOU MAY LOVE OR HATE **BRANDING.**

*But it is definitely **one of the most efficient strategies to leverage a business idea** in highly competitive markets.*

There's also co-branding, a version of branding which is being used more and more. Brand collaborates with brand. Here are some successful examples:

- Architect Rem Koolhaas's OMA (oma.eu) works with ... Prada (prada.com)
- Stella McCartney (stellamccartney.com), Karl Lagerfeld (karl-lagerfeld.com), Roberto Cavalli (robertocavalli.com) or Jimmy Choo (jimmychoo.com) work with ... H&M (hm.com)
- Lego (lego.com) collaborates with ... Muji (muji.com)
- Giorgio Armani (armanicollezioni.com) works with ... Nobu (noburestaurants.com). Actually this collaboration brings together Giorgio Armani and Nobuyuki Matsuhisa with Robert De Niro at Milan's Armani/Nobu Restaurant (armaninobu.com).

Many of you will have known these brands for years. I call them off-line brands, or b.c. brands – before connectivity – as their origin lies in traditional means of communication such as display advertisements, TV commercials and so on. But now think of what I call *a.c. brands* – the so called 'online brands' – established *after connectivity* entered our everyday lives. In 1994 the mother of all Internet sales business models, Amazon.com, was founded, followed in 1998 by Google.com, in 1999 by Blogger.com, in 2001 by Wiki-pedia.com, in 2002 by Friendster.com, MySpace.com, LinkedIn.com and OpenBC/Xing.com, in 2003 by Flickr.com, in 2004 by Facebook.com, in 2006 by Twitter.com, Behance.com, spotify.com, in 2009 by Foursquare.com, in 2010 by Pinterest and, in 2011, Google Plus. And so on. As you can see, a lot has happened in a short time – you could say we are watching online branding in its infancy. Awareness of these brands is built up through online communication and referrals – most have not even spent one cent in classical communication – but that doesn't mean their communication strategy is less efficient. Google, within its few years of its existence, has actually made it to the top ten of the most valuable global brands.[3] To understand this change in media and communication I strongly recommend you to watch *EPIC 2015* (epic. makingithappen.co.uk), a short video about the change in media and communication.

Technology and connectivity used in this way can create *long tail marketing*[4], defined by Chris Anderson, editor-in-chief of *Wired* magazine (wired.com) as a strategy that increases total sales while decreasing the cost per sale by reaching thousands of niche markets through search engine and online marketing. Traditionally, companies have tried to sell a high amount of a popular product – the idea of a blockbuster – but now with technology and connectivity we can offer and sell *small* quantities of unique products to few people. Think Amazon.com (retail), iTunes.com (music), Audible.com (audio books) and Netflix.com (video rental). Social networks such as Facebook, Linkedin, Behance or Twitter make a similar phenomenon possible for any person, from politicians to professionals. With low costs you can place your message and reach your peers wherever and whenever. What was formerly only possible for a few companies and celebrities, to build up a reputation by developing an appealing message for specific targets, is now literally possible for everyone, without any budget if they have the skills and talent. Think about Scott Schuhmann and his page thesartorialist.com, showing excellent photographs of real people on the street. His site, which receives more than a thousand visits a day, in almost no time earned such respect that he hedge hopped

BRANDING GAINS A NEW DIMENSION, ITS ONLINE DIMENSION FOR THE INDIVIDUAL!

With low costs you can place your message and reach your peers wherever and whenever.

other media in no time: he was given a monthly page in GQ (GQ. com) and video space on Style.com, published his first book and began developing many other projects.

There is also the opposite of brands: non-brands, or the so-called *'white labels'*. White labels form part of the game. They start as white labels but it is obvious that in a few years they will not be white labels any more. They grow, get a black tag and are not that cheap any more. It is a natural cycle[5]: growth, saturation, decline. So at a specific point companies need to use communication. They need to start spending money and to increase price. If not, nobody will know them and they will only compete with each other. As always in business, it's about convincing the consumer that you are the better solution. It is then that non-brands end up being brands. The Japanese retail brand Muji, for example, means *'brandless quality goods'* in Japanese, reflecting their origin as a white label.

Even if you vilify branding, remember it has been around successfully for a couple of hundred years. Don't forget the brand concept originated as consumer protection, reducing uncertainty by labelling quality and consistency. The aim now is to position and define a brand in the mind of the consumer in a way that is unique when compared to the competition. But not to be unique just for the sake of it: the uniqueness has to be relevant to people through service, experience or knowledge, for example. That is why brand positioning is a mind game. In our brain-based society perception is everything. So the behaviour of brands, like human behaviour, is one of the main drivers of a consumer's purchase decision. That is why in the offline world the retail experience is so important and the point of sale is any brand's Checkpoint Charlie[6] for authenticity, credibility and relevance. Is what is claimed about a product on TV, in magazines and online consistent with what your friends say about the product and the brand's quality? If not just don't buy the product. It is as simple as that.

The same is true in the online world. In the *a.c. (after connectivity)* age, Google has taken over from traditional media. But if your online identity is over-promising and/or doesn't fit with your offline identity – we are back to substance and style, convictions and grace – or, even worse, doesn't exist, then you will end up having problems, not selling or not getting the job. But that is fair enough.[7] A brand leverages a business idea, and its principal objective is to transmit its personality, essence and values via its visual identity.

This helps the brand to be relevant to a specific and defined target or, more precisely, a mindset. I always prefer to say mindset instead of target. The difference? Well, targets are defined by social demographics such as age, gender and income. That worked in the past. But mindset usefully reflects the idea of a state of mind based on experience, a set of beliefs or simply a mental attitude. For example, a person living in central Barcelona may have more in common with someone living in central Berlin or London than someone living 100 km outside Barcelona. Why? Because those people in central Barcelona and Berlin share experiences, they meet the same kind of people and have access to urban culture. This is a generalisation, of course, and the increasing access to information via the Internet will change this principle again, but for now it is way better, and more accurate, to work with mindsets than social demographics alone. **The final goal for any brand today is to create trust and be relevant to a defined group of people with a similar mindset.**

The positive perception of a brand combined with trust in it can be the determining thrust once people take buying decisions.

HOW SHOULD A BRAND BEHAVE? IT SHOULD JUST DO WHAT IT SAYS IT DOES!

*Trust is created by **coherent** behaviour.*

And trust is created by coherent behaviour. What does that mean? Well, a brand should do what it says it does. That counts for your off- and online identity. Always remember, like many companies, that the brand's image changes as a result of its behaviour and never before. What does that mean? Well, if you want to change the perception of a brand you can communicate a lot, but you need to prove consistently – that is, through behaviour – that your brand offer is a unique, smart and valuable solution to a specific problem. Then people will perceive, think and feel positively about it in a changed way. You could apply to branding what John Ruskin, the English writer and critic, said about quality: 'It is never an accident. It is always the result of intelligent effort.'

MANAGING RELEVANT DIFFERENCES

Branding was always used to differentiate one product from another. Think Champagne – Krug or Dom Pérignon? Both have different names, identities, behaviours, packaging, prices and ways of communicating. Each of them stands for something different. They have different points of view. Most people like either Krug or Dom Pérignon (though some would drink both without thinking twice). It is your rational and emotional perception which influences which one you buy or don't buy.

The same happens with different gin brands. I love gin and tonic. But the possibilities of drinking gin and tonic have multiplied. If you order a gin nowadays at a bar, it is a more complex scenario. You don't just get Gordon's gin as you would have done years ago. Today, in every more or less modern bar you are asked to

A BRAND ACTS LIKE A GPS, ORIENTATING AND EASING DECISIONS IN A WORLD WITH MYRIAD CHOICES.

How do you take decisions to buy one thing rather than another when you stand in front of a supermarket shelf?

choose between Bombay Sapphire (bombaysapphire.com), London (thelondon1.com), Tanqueray (tanqueray.com) or Hendrick's (hendricksgin.com), served of course with a slice of cucumber. Each taste and lifestyle has its own different solution. Each product has its supporters, each brand has its *tribe* of people with a specific mindset who believe and trust in the same thing – and that means also that each tribe has a set of brands it loves to buy. These are clearly defined and segmented little micro-cosmoses. In a world of abundance and loads of choice brands are important to orientate people. Each has its identifiable name, colours, values and behaviour. Sounds very human, right? And it is. Remember, humans can be brands, and not just soccer players or actors. And brands have two remarkable characteristics. They are *intangible*, like our own personalities, because they are more than just the physical elements of a product. And they are *intelligent* because they act like a consumer's GPS (Global Positioning System), orientating and easing decisions in a world of choices.

So differences are crucial in branding, but more specifically, the once that are relevant to people. Branding guru Marc Gobé, author of *Emotional Branding* (emotionalbranding.com) talked about this with me when I went to visit him in France last year. 'Advertising only works,' he explained, 'if the product experience and benefit you're selling people is delivered. And in most cases it's not. It seems that the more irrelevant the product, the more advertising you need. That's why design is the new advertising. It has the power to create emotional branding that lives inside people's reality.'

This is important in a world of increasing similarities with myriad choices. How do you take decisions to buy one thing rather than another when you stand in front of a supermarket shelf? Without any perceptions of difference the ideas you have about each product or service, company or person make it difficult to choose. Let's say, for example, you are either a supporter of Real Madrid (realmadrid.com) or FC Barcelona (fcbarcelona.com). Even within the category of high-class Spanish football you have different perceptions formed over years by supporters and media though that needs to be confirmed every weekend on the field. It used to be that if you loved one, you almost hated the other. On the other hand, think about Boca Juniors (bocajuniors.com.ar) in Buenos Aires and you think crazy spectators, great entertainment and ... Maradona (diegomaradona.com). Branding is the management of such differences, especially between very similar offers. All supporters of one club share their perception of it: they trust in their players, they hope to see them playing great games and win trophies. This, which is called brand conviction, has been growing over many years. Authentic behaviour is what defines those brands. Something similar is happening in fashion. What makes ladies put their names on waiting lists to get a Hermès (hermes.com) 'Kelly' bag (named after Grace Kelly) or a 'Birkin' bag (named after actress Jane Birkin) for a large amount of money – at prices which begin at around $7,000 and can go well beyond $50,000 – when they could easily buy a nice car for that amount? These products stand for something people want: a bag full of exclusivity, style, quality, joy and history. Ladies want this bag, nothing else and nothing less.

Think also about Cirque du Soleil (cirquedusoleil.com). What is it really? A circus? A show? A theatre? Or a musical? Where and with whom does it compete? It is difficult to say. But it opened up a new market, using a '*blue ocean strategy*', as authors W. Chan Kim and Renée Mauborgne call it in their book of the same title. In other words, instead of bloodily fighting it out with too many competitors in an overpopulated red ocean you opt for a strategy where you open a new market with no competitors by swimming out towards an empty blue ocean. This is important in a world of increasing similarities. The brand idea is one that makes you confident to make the right choice in a consumer world with many different possibilities. But what is even better is how Guy Laliberté, the founder of Cirque du Soleil, had the opportunity to leverage Cirque du Soleil himself and show his original skills and ideas around the world. The brand can, and does, very successfully cater to 100 million spectators through twenty shows running simultaneously in 300 cities worldwide.

TELL A GOOD STORY – YOURS!

If a brand convinces a tribe that its consistent quality, unique value and special service is worth the money then the brand is on the sunny side of branding. Communication of identity is the key driving force behind efficiency. There are, of course, also non-brands which enjoy great success because they provide a more economical offer for similar standards. If customers cannot perceive a clear benefit for the premium paid for a brand it will get into real trouble. This is increasingly the case with brands run by inexperienced, short-sighted and quarterly result-driven managers and with companies that are not used to working with branding.

Think healthcare. For many years there were monopolies with no competition at all. Most patents running today were given in the 1970s and 1980s. But now, thirty years later, many of these patents are running out. That is why you now find, side by side in the same pharmacy, 'me-too' products with the same active ingredients

IN ANY CASE, THE COMMUNICATION OF YOUR IDENTITY IS THE KEY DRIVER OF EFFICIENCY!

Take care, you are communicating, even if you are not saying anything.

as more expensive neighbouring brands. Healthcare companies just didn't think it was necessary to mention who originally invested the money to develop the product – sometimes for decades – and who performed the safety and security tests to offer a 100% safe and secure product. It is also strange that few people are surprised by how these companies are valued so badly on the stock market. How can it be that pharmaceutical company shares are much cheaper on the stock market than those of companies producing FMCG? Here I mean *fast-moving consumer goods*, in other words frequently purchased goods such as snacks or soft drinks? Well, people just don't trust healthcare companies. Too many people have a negative perception of them. Over the last decade they have started to use branding in order to differentiate themselves and communicate who they are, what they do and why that matters. They started well, but as a whole, the industry now seems to be more interested in M&A – Mergers and Acquisitions – so their identities are further blurring and fading away among employees, doctors and patients.

Your story, well told, will influence the perception of your product. You are communicating, even if you are not saying anything. As Paul Watzlawick, the Austrian-American psychologist and philosopher, says about communication: '*you cannot not communicate*'. Communication is really complex, and not even a lifetime is enough to master it fully. Words form around 7% of interpersonal communication, tonality 38% and body language 55%. Think about communication with your family, your husband or wife, your friends, your neighbours, your boss, your clients, your colleagues. Think about how they talk, the tone and the words they use, the message and content they convey. How many times have you said or heard someone say: 'I really don't understand you'. **There is a big difference between being listened to, being heard and being understood.**

For brands, communication is often a question of life or death. In our highly competitive environments brands need to behave and communicate as Scheherazade did to the Sultan of Persia in *A Thousand and One Nights*. Sultan Shahryar found his first wife had been unfaithful and, after deciding that he hated all women, he married and killed a new wife each day. Scheherazade, in an effort to avoid his previous wives' fate, told him a fascinating story every night, promising to finish it the following night. The Sultan enjoyed the stories so much that he put off her execution indefinitely and finally abandoned the idea altogether. Successful brands work with the same method. Authentic, credible, exciting and relevant stories told well each day, at each moment, at each consumer touch point[8], are the secret to their survival.

THINKING AND DOING

I should say here that the word *'strategy'* is bandied about a lot. It always sounds good, in every speech or presentation, but it does not always make sense. We call concepts 'strategic concepts', decisions 'strategic decisions', investments 'strategic investments', and so on, when most of these things are just tactics.

Therefore bear in mind three important things about strategy:

1. A strategy is a plan of action designed to achieve a particular goal.
2. Strategy is long term, tactics are short term. You don't change

your strategy every day!

3. You can never split strategy from implementation (from doing things).

That said, strategic planning is of interest for every individual's communication. Many of today's well-known actors, soccer players, writers and politicians have a strategic communication plan. Why? It provides direction and meaning. You know where you want to go. This eliminates doubts, eases decisions in daily life and therefore positively affects your future. You can focus your strength, time, energy (and of course money), leverage and skills on your most important opportunities, thus significantly increasing results and, undoubtedly, enhancing your quality of life.

Strategic planning – analysing a situation and evaluating the options to reach a defined goal in complex and ever-changing environments – is fundamental in branding. It aims to define the fundamentals on which you will take decisions and define actions that further shape your future based on 'who you are', 'where you want to go', 'what you do', 'when you will do it' and 'how you will do it'. Great books about strategy like Sun Tzu's *The Art of War* (more than 2,500 years old!) or Carl Von Clausewitz's *On War* refer to its military origin but nowadays they have become popular business books.

You will have started to learn how to develop strategy in earlier chapters. Understanding our personality by identifying our potential, interests and motivations forms the basis for developing strategies. Equally, strategy without creativity is nothing. **Strategy doesn't work in a team which shares objectives but not values.** This is especially true in collaborations where each of the members take decisions based on different values. If the environment is a very important issue to you, but not for the others in your team, you will end up going your separate ways, even though you have a common goal.

There are two other points to be made here. First, it doesn't make sense to define a strategy which cannot be implemented with the available resources. That means if you don't have the time, the money or the skills to develop that great film you want to get made it is not very good strategy to put a lot of energy into it. That doesn't mean you have to give up the idea of making a film altogether, but maybe aim at a low-budget short film that is more focused on concept and idea rather than on special effects and amazing locations.

Secondly, strategy is the plan, but you also need real action. Bear in mind that the average person who acts is much more successful than the genius who doesn't act. But acting without thinking is a waste of time. **Thinking and doing are equally important.** Otherwise we belong to those who have great ideas, but will never ever get them off the ground.

PERSONAL BRANDING IN THE AGE OF CONNECTIVITY

So now let's look at strategies and planning tactics for communicating your substance and your style, your conviction and your grace online and offline. And how to put them into action now. More than ever you need to define a plan and structured approach to market yourself, using the intangible and intelligent. Planning is a kind of rain dance. It will most probably not bring rain, but it will definitely make you a much better dancer. It prepares you for all kinds of deviations. It is the only way to find out if you are on track or off it. It is the only way to find out, if you are off track, how you can get back on it. I am not talking about a superficial and over-promising approach. I am talking about a proven methodology to structure and organise highly complex systems and environments. You and your working-life ideas can be easily called complex systems.

1. THINK DIFFERENTLY ABOUT YOURSELF

Now think differently about yourself. This is the part where the strategy meets reality. What makes you different? You have identified your potential, your passion, your substance and convictions. So what is your product or service? Where are you in the market? Are you online or offline? You are aware that it is really important to use your creativity. You now also know your strategy comes from your personality.

Now look for feedback. Does your product or service light up the eyes of your potential clients as well as the existing ones? If not, rethink your product. What have you done lately to stand out professionally? Do your peers and stakeholders know it? Your boss, customer, husband, wife, friends, colleagues? Or are you still blurry to them? Does the CEO or the human resources manager of the company you are working for, or you want to work with, know about you and your specific qualities? Does he know your identity, vision, mission and values? Does he understand your point of view, your experience and the extent of your knowledge? Were you able to convey it during the last interviews, or at the last assessment session? Did he find an article written by you about a specific topic relevant for the job you want to be in? Or a speech you gave at a conference? Or on the website you've created about your subject? Remember your online presence today often presents your first impression on people, which you then need to confirm 'live'. As an individual you are more than the bits and bytes that form you. The perception other people have of you, starting with your name, helps your peers to differentiate you. The secret is to transmit coherently the quality of your substance, your unique offer and special service to your peers.

If you are not sure about these yourself how can you expect other people to be? Have you made no effort to differentiate yourself in the market? To acquire specific skills? To understand market needs? Well, wouldn't it be prudent to give it a serious shot and use the brand concept for yourself? Wouldn't it make sense to combine creativity and strategy, off- and online, to use the intangible intelligently?

Choices have multiplied in all markets and the job market is no exception. A human resources manager responsible for recruitment today has more choices than ever. In all the companies that I had or worked for, I always recruited staff personally because I think of it as a key management responsibility, especially in service companies where the only thing that really counts are the people. Well, the fact is that for every single job you offer you receive literally hundreds or even thousands of CVs. How can I choose? How can other people responsible for recruiting in much larger companies with even more job candidates make their choice? How can you choose the perfect collaborator or partner? What does it mean for you? Well, you have competition wherever you see. Direct (similar profile) and indirect (different profile). Known and unknown. Better, faster, and many times cheaper. There is now total competition.

2. CREATE TRUST AND CONFIDENCE

Branding is the management of differences in the minds of people. Branding is even more important in the new economy where choices have multiplied and total competition is the norm. Branding has gained new importance in the age of connectivity. But the rules are the same. The secret is to create trust and confidence. It is complicated, but the aim is to get into people's hearts and minds. Why not in the hearts and minds of those people relevant to you? The ones who decide if you get the job, or not. Or those who are close to the ones who take the decisions? But keep in mind that *attention,* next to time, is the scarcest commodity of the 21st century.

Nobody is waiting for you, nobody will call you. YOU need to move. That's the key for every sales person. And you need to deliver what you promise. Do you hand in your work on time? Do the internal and external clients get a reliable service from you? Do you anticipate problems and find solutions to them? Does your client save money by having you on the project? Do you complete projects on budget?

Don't tell me you have nothing to sell. You have and you should. Everybody lives by selling something. That is why you need a methodology to position yourself in an overcrowded marketplace – one that is straightforward, filled with fun and joy and that can consistently build up over time to be credible, genuine and unique.

3. BE AWARE OF THE PITFALLS IN EXPOSING YOUR ONLINE IDENTITY

Of course you cannot control the whole process, but you can influence your peers and stakeholders by communicating to them the expertise and qualities that make you different. Some enthusiasts praise social networks for presenting chances for identity-play and see opportunities for all of us to be an online celebrity with the unique possibility to change this identity whenever we want to, without any risk and consequences. Not true.

Even the youngest of us will look for a job sooner or later and the human resources manager will Google him or her. The creation and consumption of intimate details and images of one's own and others' lives is the main activity on online social networks. It's somehow a dramatic form of *solipsism*, a philosophical idea that only one's own mind is certain to exist. Social networks are still in their infancy, and we are growing with them, but sometimes we are not aware of the amount of intimate details and information we are making publicly available.

This carelessness can be dangerous. In the offline world you wouldn't give strangers your telephone number and tell them intimate details and secrets, but online you give this information out to the whole world. And when one's darker side finds expression in a virtual space, privacy becomes difficult and that private misbehaviour becomes public exhibitionism. You take the decisions. I am just here to reflect the reality. Employers will definitely Google your website, blog and social network profiles as part of their hiring process. Social networks such as Linkedin (linkedin.com), XING (xing.com) and, for the creative community, especially Behance (behance.com), are specifically for job search, but your identity should be integral to them. If you reach the stage where they can identify you, find possibilities to locate relevant information about you – not just those amusing weekend pictures on Facebook – and clear statements of your expertise and experience, they will then perceive you differently. You need them to see that you have an interesting point of view, a good product or service for an acceptable price and, what is more, a great attitude.

VISUALISE THE ESSENCE OF YOUR IDENTITY

After the exhausting thought processes of the personality chapter – thinking about vision, mission, values, your goals and objectives – it is time once again to create. This time you have to combine both parts of your brain and apply your logical thinking, imagination and passion to the conclusions of your various learning experiences. Your website or your blog, your business card or anything else should always have its deep roots in aesthetics. The first step is visibility. It's difficult at the start and difficult to make it professional, but you get a lot of credit and kudos if you are an expert.

How can you communicate who you are to the people relevant to you? How can you express it even if you are not talking to them in person? This section wants to suggest your visual identity can do much of that for you. Your visual identity comprises all visible elements of your work identity: name or logo, fonts and colours applied to your stationery (business card and email signature, letterhead, etc.), presentation templates (for PowerPoint or Keynote), blog and/or website and profiles on social network sites. Your office, its design and architecture, should also be part of your visual identity. The same applies to your physical appearance. Actually everything counts, online and offline, that visually communicates who you are, what you do and why it should matter to mindset-specific peers. Your visual identity is an essential part of the process of creative personal branding that enables you to build your reputation and enhance your profile. To create a strong and efficient brand you need to apply it consistently across all of your communication. Put passion and enthusiasm into it and you will get your investment of emotional and intellectual energy back in a big way. Why is visual communication so powerful? Well, our brain responds more strongly to visual communication and this therefore adds an extra dimension to your verbal credentials.

Once you have developed your visual identity you can spend your time improving and updating content rather than developing another template and hunting for the right font each time you need to give a presentation. One more suggestion: remember when I mentioned that creativity is very social? So is your visual identity. Even if you are good at it, you need another point of view. Ask a professional designer to help you with it. Yes, it will cost you money. But it's worth it. It will guarantee a better result, be more efficient and will definitely look more professional.

Let's start with your logo. Your logo means your identity, your speech and your meaning. The logo and especially the logotype (a stylized type) should give your peers the possibility to identify you and differentiate you from your competitors.

Your font is also very important. Historically there are two different types, serif typefaces such as Garamond or Bodoni, or sans serif typefaces such as Univers, Helvetica or Futura. Today you have many new and visually pleasing types. But a word of caution: be aware of how to use them. I was lucky to be taught typography by pedantic teachers trained and influenced by the philosophy of the *Bauhaus*, the modernist architecture and design movement founded by Walter Gropius and later directed by Mies van der Rohe and the Swiss School of Typography, often known as the Swiss Style – now you now why the typeface is called Helvetica. They forced us to reconstruct a print-ready version of an entire alphabet – Bauer Bodoni – by hand in black and white, working it out from only three given letters. This was based on our capacity to see, understand and reconstruct the form and especially the proportion between black and white. This zen-like meditational work trains you to see the beauty and aesthetics of a well-designed logotype, poster or book.

Colour is important too. It tells a lot about you, it evokes emotion and creates strong brand recognition. Maybe you have already been given a specific colour or two from your peers in your feedback test? That would be great. If not just go to your wardrobe and see what kind of colours you have there. Normally just two or three. If you are interested, read books about colours and their significance. There is a lot of literature on the subject, from Harald Küppers' *The Basic Law of Colour Theory*, Johann Wolfgang von Goethe's *Theory of Colours* to work on colours in psychology.

Finally come the slogan and the images you put with your identity. A slogan is a memorable and motivational tagline. Just remember Barack Obama's 'Yes, we can'. It has a lot to do with your mission statement and purpose. **Express your core values.**

'Images of yourself' are always a tricky thing. As with fonts and presentations, a professional eye is important. As almost everybody has an Apple computer and a digital camera, we all think we can take great photographs like Helmut Newton (helmutnewton.com), Terry Richardson (terrysdiary.com) or Mario Testino (mariotestino.com). That's not true. Many of the people around me have lots of pictures but, I'm sorry to say, at least 80% are not good, not even close to good.

One rule on images. An amateur, if he is lucky, takes *one* great shot out of hundred, a professional *three* to five. Remember:

1. Photography is an art.
2. A professional photographer is three to five times more likely to take a great shot than you.
3. Digital cameras support quantity and do not guarantee quality.

A consistent use of images can help you to connect to your peers and clients. Think about using a professional photographer or your designer.

Assignment — 7:
DEVELOP YOUR VISUAL
IDENTITY

You need to define the key elements of your visual identity you want, so start now with the next few assignments.

My suggestion When you choose a designer, pick one who is likely to understand you and your business and has the potential to develop a style you feel you identify with. Agree on a deadline and ask how many design options and revisions will be included (normally three).

1 — Your Logo

a) Look at examples of logos you like. El Bulli restaurant (elbulli. com), where chef Ferran Adrià cooked, is one good source. See his logo and compare it to those of other restaurants you know. It is different, it communicates all you need to know – personality, character, creativity, heritage, passion – and besides that it tells a graceful story, as it pays homage to the French bulldog, a breed known as 'bulli', owned by the former owners of the restaurant, a family called Schillings. Funnily enough the name of the well-known English restaurant, The Fat Duck (fatduck.co.uk), also triggers a story in your mind and it's difficult to forget the name.

b) Do some first sketches of your own logo.

2 — *Your Font*

a) Look at samples of work given awards by the type directors club (tdc.org), an organisation devoted to excellence in typography.

b) To train yourself compare different logos and typefaces, like that of fashion designer Stella McCartney (stellamccartney.com) to Stefan Sagmeister (sagmeisterwalsh.com), photographer David Lachapelle (lachapellestudio.com) or designer Tokujin Yoshioka (tokujin.com).

What is your perception? In your opinion do their choices transmit who they are, what they do and why it matters?

c) Think about which logos and typefaces you prefer.

3 — Your Colour

a) Shortlist two to three colours that you believe reflect you, and most importantly, with which you feel comfortable.

---

b) Ask your designer to help you with this task. Ask him for feedback.

4 — Your Slogan

a) Go back to our mission statement and use it as a base to develop a slogan which should be 'easy to remember, motivational and different' to the one of your competitors.

---

5 — Your Images

a) Review all the pictures you have of yourself. Select three and ask your peers what they think about those pictures. Do they represent an expression of you? Do they express your values? Consider that possibly they do not.

b) Write down where you keep the high-resolution pictures you like.

_____

_____

_____

_____

_____

COMMUNICATE AND CONNECT

Now let's turn to your marketing and communication. Here you will apply your visual identity. What are your communication channels and measures? What do you need? What are the things you've always wanted? I would say there are three different and really important communication measures. As all measures go hand in hand nowadays, and it is not a question of either-or, I will not distinguish between on- and offline elements.

First, for example, is your *stationery*. This is a basic must-have that goes way beyond printed stationery today. This means your business card and your email signature, your website and blog, your letterhead, your invoice, your envelopes, labels, thank-you cards and, of course, your presentation template (as you will present many times in your life, believe me).

Especially important is your email signature, which will reach more people than your business card. An ideal email template generally includes the following: the company's logo, the sender's signature, a link to the company's website and the company's legal information, which includes registration number, place of registration, and registered office address as well as the legal disclaimer (emaildisclaimer.com). We are used to putting this information on our letterhead, but most of us forget that the same applies to email.

This has started to become a legal requirement in many countries. In the UK, for example, it has become mandatory since 1 January 2007. Please also think about protecting your creative products, your logo, name, ideas and designs and make sure that you have copyrights, trademarks or patents registered. Remember handsoffmydesign.com, the website about European Union Design Protection.

A credential is an attestation or showcase of your substance, competence, skills, capabilities and accomplishments, your best-cases portfolio, your conviction, philosophy (vision, mission and values), client references, articles and the awards you have received in your career. It should contain the most relevant content that will help you make potential clients confident enough to give you the job, and could possibly take the form of a book, a folder, a presentation, a video or a website, or an effective combination of all or some of them.

Your credentials have to present your personal website, blog or both where anyone can access and get a quick overview of who you are and what you have to offer. It is the first thing people like to do today.

Assignment — 8:
DEVELOP YOUR MARKETING COMMUNICATION

1 — Stationery

a) Define the five most important measures of your stationery. Think online and offline.

_____

_____

_____

_____

_____

b) Ask a designer or other visual professional for feedback.

2 — Credentials

My personal tip: Don't neglect your online portfolio, but equally, don't forget offline media, as people love a well-designed and properly printed book, folder or a thank-you card.

a) Define your credentials now.

_____

_____

_____

_____

_____

b) Focus on content and efficiency.

SOCIAL CAPITAL AND SOCIAL NETWORKS

As collaboration is an absolutely key skill it makes sense to treat it with the appropriate respect. It is about how people can connect to you, find you on different platforms and get information about you. More than 60% of all jobs are found through networking, and word of mouth is one of the best marketing tools ever.

Remember that the first thing people will do is to Google you. Then they will go to social network sites to get more information about you. As I mentioned before, this new connectivity links everyone with everyone. It is the basic idea behind all social network sites. According to the *six degrees of separation* principle, each person is separated from another person by fewer than six degrees.

The idea grew out of a study about social connections called *small world experiment* in 1967 by Harvard sociologist and psychologist Stanley Milgram. He asked 160 students to post chain letters and trace their journey to a particular target person not personally known to them. He found out that the average number of 5.5 connections (intermediate acquaintance links) were needed to connect them. In 2003 Duncan J. Watson, a professor at Columbia University and author of *Six Degrees: The Science of a Connected Age*, repeated Milgram's experiment by using a website asking 61,000 people to send messages to 18 targets worldwide. He confirmed Milgram's result. We live in a small world, where everyone can be linked to everyone else. But obviously we don't only want to know how closely we are connected – we also want to know what kinds of communities and friendships we are creating.

One very important point here: the quality of your social capital is more important than quantity, and by quality I mean how

THE MORE YOU RESPECT YOUR PRIVATE SPHERE, THE MORE YOU RESPECT YOURSELF!

And please, only hand out personal information when requested, not on every single occasion that social networking sites offers you.

much you like to deal with people. If you focus on quality instead of the number of people in your network, you are more likely to reach good results while having fun along the way. And *please*, only hand out personal information when requested, not on every single occasion that social networking sites offers you. The more you respect your private sphere, the more you respect yourself.

Social networks offer a great opportunity to find *like-minded people*. They give you the possibility to find out more about specific themes that interest you, who else is working on them, and who could be interesting to work with. You also find information about events and festivals, awards, schools and institutions. Another great way to get into contact with people with similar thinking to you is through public relations specialists. Besides internet PR (public relations) you can also use those trained in marketing-communication discipline. There are many different special-interest magazines, which could be interesting for you to reach a specific target and which maybe are interested in interviewing you as an expert. PR specialists can help you to find these magazines and are well versed in connecting and developing content jointly with you for them.

Assignment — 9:
ADAPTING COMMUNICATIONS TO YOUR NEEDS

My idea is that you need to focus on the most efficient ways to position yourself in a highly (and increasingly demanding) competitive environment.

My personal suggestion Analyse which ways can first create opportunities, and then help you to grow personally and finally visualise and verbalise the difference between you and your competition.

a) Define your social capital and which social networks can transmit your message coherently and credibly. Write out a report, as if for a client.

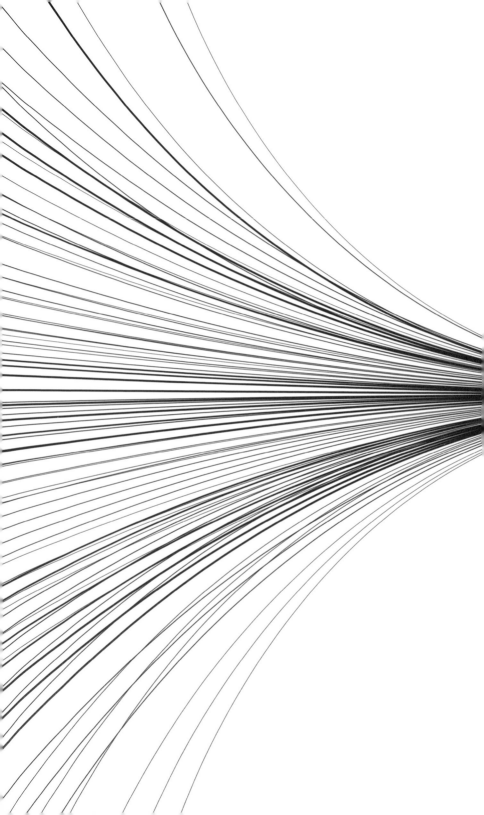

06
_GO!

Where Next?

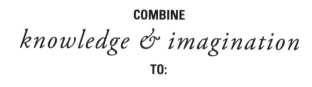

COMBINE

knowledge & imagination

TO:

01 — GO! — REFLECT!

02 — REFRAME!

03 — CREATE!

04 — GROW!

05 — DIFFERENTIATE!

06 — BRANDING / PERSONAL / CREATIVE

ALWAYS WITH

substance, style, conviction and grace.

Evaluate where you are every six months – creating, growing, differentiating? Repeat the CPB process. Enjoy it. You will find yourself driven by priorities. You will also have stress in your life, but positive stress. You will be able to do much more and you will feel good about it. You will set yourself goals which are achievable. Bear in mind that hyperactivity, super-busy and 'more' are not goals. Productivity driven by passion is a goal, though, as is sustainability. You must take charge as a creative leader, taking decisions based on your values to make change possible and positively impact society and the economy.

Wouldn't that be great? This is what CPB aims to give you – creative leadership. If you combine creative thinking with your knowledge and experience, and if you structure it and define it, the results can be astonishing. If you have an idea NOW, go for it. Don't worry about other people and what they think. They don't think properly that often anyway, and will be all too quick to try and demotivate you. Once you reach your full momentum, however, they will get out of your way. Don't waste any time. There is no such thing as 'when the time is right'.

Some day is today.

START NOW

And, above all,

ENJOY!

CREATIVE PERSONAL BRANDING—NOTES

NOTES

My interest in personal branding was sparked by an article by Tom Peters, entitled 'The Brand Called You', published in Fast Company in 1997. I first discovered it four years later when I started to apply my marketing, branding and communication techniques, learned over the previous decade, to sports people and actors. I quickly realised its potential within our new creative economy, as I felt the general perception of personal branding as simply selling was a mistaken one, but I included creativity and creative thinking as key elements of CPB 'to take it a step forward'.

1 REFLECT!

1. A hypermarket is a superstore which combines a supermarket and a department store. Examples are those run by Carrefour in Europe, Wal-Mart in the USA (where they are known as Supercenters), or Tesco in England. Carrefour hypermarkets stock an average of 70,000 items and their floor area ranges from approximately 5,000 to 20,000 sq. m. (according to businessweek.com).

2. See recent developments in unemployment at a European and Member State level: (epp.eurostat.ec.europa.eu/statistics_explained/index.php/Unemployment_statistics), December 2012.

3. A record number of 204 teams entered the preliminary competition (Fifa.com, 30 March 2007).

4. See World Trade Organisation figures on world trade expansion: (www.wto.org/english/tratop_e/envir_e/climate_impact_e.htm)

5. See Joia Shillingford's interview with Dave Evans for her article 'Computers to be "aware"', *Financial Times,* 17 September 2008.

6. The World Intellectual Property Organisation (Wipo.int), on the other hand, states, 'creative industries has a wider meaning and includes, besides the cultural industries, all cultural or artistic production, whether live or produced as an individual unit and is traditionally used in relation to live performances, cultural heritage and similar high-art activities.' The UK Government department for Culture, Media and Sports (DCMS 2001, culture.gov.uk) describes the creative industries as: 'those industries which have their origin in individual creativity, skill and talent and which have a potential for wealth and job creation through the generation and exploitation of intellectual property.' The current DCMS definition recognises eleven creative sectors: Advertising, Architecture, Arts and Antique Markets, Crafts, Design, Fashion, Film/Video/Photography, Software/Computer Games, Electronic Publishing, Music/Visual and Performing Arts, Publishing, Television and Radio.
See also: http://www.internetworldstats.com/stats.htm (30 June 2012).

7. José Manuel Durão Barroso, President of the European Commission, in *Europe 2020: A strategy for smart, sustainable and inclusive growth*, 25–26 March 2010. For commentary on the digital society, see p.10. Every page of the full report, which can be downloaded from http://ec.europa.eu/eu2020/index_en.htm is worth reading to gain a picture of the impact of the crisis and the European Commission's plans to work on it.

2 REFRAME!

1. Boo.com, one of my favourite online case studies for students, is the mother of all online fashion retail companies. Its extraordinary 'burn rate' of spending on advertising and promotion totalled around $135 million of venture capital in just 18 months. Founder Ernst Malmsten's book *boo hoo* is worth reading or, if the book is too long, read the article about it on http://www.guardian.co.uk/technology/2005/may/16/media.business.

2. Norberto Gallego, 'Kodak – Cinco años de reconversión ... y sigue', *La Vanguardia*, 2 May 2010.

3. United Nations Conference on Trade and Development, *Creative Economy Report* 2010, p.190 'A Feasible Development Option' (unctad.org.).

4. Thanks to John Hawkins the creative economy is a common term in Australia, Asia – especially in Shanghai – and Europe. See his book *The Creative Economy: How People Make Money from Ideas*, Penguin, 2001. I interviewed him in London in December 2009. See also www.creativeeconomy.com

5. Richard Florida, *The Rise of the Creative Class and How It's Transforming Work, Leisure, Community and Everyday Life*, Basic Books, 2002. Thanks to him there is an ongoing debate about a positive interaction between society and the city that has helped many cities to change their point of view about the importance of what Florida calls the three Ts: Technology, Talent and Tolerance.

6. José Manuel Durão Barroso, President of the European Commission, *Europe 2020: A strategy for smart, sustainable and inclusive growth*: page 5, entitled 'A moment of Transformation'. The crisis has wiped out recent progress (25–26 March 2010). This is a must-read!

7. The US Bureau of Labor Statistics, http://www.bls.gov/emp/, was very helpful in supplying information to compare. They have a Employment Projections Program and as a result a Projection Summary 2008–2018 as well as an Occupational Outlook Handbook and Career Guide to Industries. See http://www.bls.gov/oco/oco2003.htm

8. European Reference Framework, Eight Key Competences for Lifelong Learning. (I didn't know this existed until I talked to Commissioner Jan Figel about the future of work and life and he mentioned the Eight Key Competences.)

The European Parliament's and Council's recommendations are outcomes of the European Commission's and Member States' work within the Education and Training 2010 Work Programme. (See ec.europa.eu/dgs/education_culture/publ/pdf/ll.../keycomp_en.pdf).

3 CREATE!

1. I had the chance to listen and talk to Edward de Bono at the executive meeting for EADA Alumni at the Hotel Arts, Barcelona in 2009. Here he talked about the GG3, the 'Greek Gang of Three' and their long-term influence on western thought: Socrates, Plato and Aristotle. Socrates, he said, was interested in dialectic argument and questions to find the truth. Aristotle, he said, put things in boxes. When Greek thinking came to Europe during the Renaissance schools, university and thinking in general were in the hands of the church and therefore based on faith. There was no need for creative or design thinking. What people needed instead was truth, logic and argument to prove religious theories wrong. This became the basis of western thinking, aimed at finding the truth. But de Bono argues we have never really developed the very different thinking that is required for creating value.

2. Sandra Aamodt and Sam Wang, *Welcome to Your Brain*, Why You Lose Your Car Keys but Never Forget How to Drive and Other Puzzles of Everyday Life, Bloomsbury New York, 2008. We need to know how the brain works, and this book is clear, understandable, entertaining and fascinating, and written by two top neuroscientists. To get a first idea go to their blog: welcometoyourbrain.com

3. Daniel H. Pink, *A Whole New Mind*, Why Right-Brainers Will Rule the World, Riverhead Books, 2005. This book helped me understand my own ways of thinking as a designer with an MBA and made me want to learn more about the impact of the way we educate.

4. I tried to research this story, which I heard years ago, but couldn't find any proof for it. Anyway I like the story. See also http://en.wikipedia.org/wiki/Necktie.

5. TBWA/Chiat Day also produced '1984', the most famous Apple advertisement and probably the most famous commercial ever, directed by Ridley Scott. If you haven't seen it watch it on http://www.youtube.com/watch?v=HhsWzJo2sN4

6. Milan's Domus Academy (domusacademy.com) collaborates with the Bocconi University (unibocconi.eu) in that city on its Master in Business Design course. http://www.domusacademy.com/businessdept). Insead (insead.edu) works with campuses in Fontainebleau (France) and Singapore and collaborates with Pasadena Art Center (artcenter.edu). Other great steps in the right direction include: the Master in Design Management at IED (http://www.iedbarcelona.es/en/pedagogical_areas/design-management-only-in-english_46.html) in Barcelona, for the time being the only Master in Design Management in Spain, which combines business and creativity, teaches design thinking and creative leadership; the Master in Design Thinking at the Institute of Design, Stanford (http://dschool.stanford.edu/), California; the MA in Innovation Management at Central Saint Martin's College of Art & Design, London (http://www.csm.arts.ac.uk/courses/postgraduate/innovation-management.htm). All these courses try to allow creative and business thinking to meet and serve the new requirements of the new creative economy. This change in thinking will take at least a generation: business schools are still too focused on exploiting businesses instead of creating sustainable, human- and eco-friendly businesses, and most design schools, especially in Europe, still concentrate too much on creativity for its own sake rather than on empathy and understanding the needs and wants of clients and consumers.

7. Social entrepreneurship is the work of a social entrepreneur. A social entrepreneur is someone who recognizes a social problem and uses entrepreneurial principles to organize, create, and manage a venture to bring about social change. (http://en.wikipedia.org/wiki/Social_entrepreneurship)

8. Creativity and Innovation European Year 2009 (www.create2009.europa.eu). A great initiative, great programmes and great ambassadors, but few people were aware of it.

9. Creative entrepreneurs combine creativity and business aspects of their area of interest, a skill which is mandatory in the increasingly flexible structure peculiar to the creative economy. That is why it is so important to understand and be familiar with organising your own and other talent (salaries, contracts, working conditions etc.), financing (access to credit and funding), protection of rights (copyright and see also note 9 below), technology (creating, producing and distribution), knowledge upgrading etc.

10. Intellectual property ('IP') rights are the legal rights which protect creations of the human mind (yours), covering all kinds of creative areas such as inventions, designs and different kinds of artistic expression, as well as other more commercial areas like trade marks and trade secrets.

11. Value-chain analysis is one of the most widely recognised methods for analysing the structure of creative industries and creative production chains from inception to after-service. It makes sense to understand your own value chain as it gives you the possibility to understand and optimise your role in it.

12. When I teach communication I always integrate a social communication assignment and find almost all students love to apply their knowledge to a good cause.

13. Service design is a structured approach to improve quality and interaction between a service provider and customers. It is a primary focus for design management students.

14. Ethnographic research has evolved from observational research. It is a method where consumers are tracked in their natural environment (e.g. at home) to analyse their decision and usage patterns concerning specific products.

4 GROW!

1. Sometimes also called the Millennial Generation, Generation Y is defined as those who were born after 1984, and was digital from day one. This generation lives and loves social networks and any kind of digital communication. My personal experience is that they are all over the place – physically, virtually and mentally – and are culturally very tolerant, multilingual, with a high understanding of information and brand culture. They know a lot about many different topics, they are much more practical as Generation X and prefer pictures and colours to words. They also love new ideas and companies with relevant philosophies. Their attention span is very short, they have little patience and they want to have everything now.

2. The generation born between 1965 and 1984 is called Generation X. The term was popularised by Canadian author Douglas Coupland's 1991 novel *Generation X: Tales for an Accelerated Culture*, describing the generation's lifestyle. This generation (and I am one of them) lived through the end of the Cold War but still thinks in terms of left- and right-wing politics. Their working parents, sometimes divorced, have made them independent. They saw the beginning of the digital age, TV going from black and white to colour, the birth of millions of blogs and the dramatic influence of AIDS on their sex lives. They are highly influenced by pop culture from Billy Idol to Michael Jackson, Pearl Jam and Tupac to Madonna, especially via MTV. They react to discovery, travel, creativity, inspiration and lifestyle brands. They are a small generation: half of the number of baby boomers and half of Generation Y (see note 4 below).

3. According to a year-long study conducted by McKinsey Co. in 1997 the most important corporate resource due to demographic and social changes over the next twenty years will be talent. (http://www.fastcompany.com/magazine/16/mckinsey.html)

4. Baby boomers are the generation born in the period following the Second World War, from 1946 to 1964. They lived through the assassinations of JFK,

Malcolm X and Martin Luther King; they saw Neil Armstrong's first steps on the moon on TV; they were influenced by the Vietnam War, Woodstock and the sexual revolution of the 1960s, the Beatles and Jimi Hendrix. As a group double the size of Generation X, they grew up genuinely expecting the world to improve with time. They react to success based on hard work, they love social status and heroes, they like convenience, luxury and anti-ageing products and services.

5. See Alicia Clegg, 'In search of a life after redundancy', *Financial Times* (25 September 2008). Clegg writes about the possibility of redundancy awakening a latent talent for entrepreneurship. 'Research based on psychometric tests by Proteus Consultancy, a UK career management organisation, suggests as few as 9 per cent of people work in careers or workplaces suited to their personality'.

6. Bear in mind the '*Pareto principle*', also called the '80–20 rule', named after Italian economist Vilfredo Pareto, which states that roughly 80% of output comes from 20% input. Applied to most businesses, this means that 80% of their sales come from 20% of their clients. The other hint I would like to give you is Parkinson's Law, according to which the demand upon a resource tends to expand to match the supply of the resource. In my own words and in my experience this describes how the longer the time you have to spend on a project (your thesis for example), the bigger it gets mentally.

7. Peer pressure is a phenomenon that exists for all ages. It refers to a social group's influence in encouraging an individual to change attitude, values or behaviour. Sometimes a person is pulled between the desire to be seen as an individual of unique values and the desire to belong to a group where he or she feels accepted.

8. A lot has been said and written about coaching. Today, though it is not a protected job and anybody can call themselves a coach. It is a recognised discipline used by professionals engaged in human development focused on

achieving results. Professional coaching is not therapy. A professional coach may apply mentoring, personal experience, expertise and encouragement, values assessment, behaviour modelling, goal-setting and other techniques, depending on their experience in helping clients. In general a coach helps to identify a client's skills and capabilities and enables them to use them to the best of their ability for empowerment towards specific goals. Personally I think it is one of the best investments you can make in your life, but it is important to choose the right coach with the right experience and attitude.

9. Omega Speedmaster Professional, the legendary 'Moon Watch' worn by Buzz Aldrin when he stepped on to the Moon in July 1969. The idea that human beings were capable of reaching the Moon defined my own philosophy: it made me think that a lot is possible if you want it. I bought this watch on my 30th birthday and I still enjoy wearing it. http://www.omegawatches.com/spirit/hall-of-fame/watches/the-legendary-moonwatch

10. *Kaizen*, the Japanese word for 'continuous improvement', refers to a philosophy for constantly optimising manufacturing processes successfully applied by companies like Toyota.

11. An oath is either a statement of fact or a promise invoking something or someone that the oath maker considers sacred – often, in western cultures, God – as a witness to the binding nature of the promise or the truth of the statement of fact. To swear is to take an oath. See http://en.wikipedia.org/wiki/Oath or www.thunderbird.edu/about_thunderbird/inside_tbird/oath_of_honor.htm

12. Corporate Social Responsibility (CSR), according to the European Commission's definition, is: 'A concept whereby companies integrate social and environmental concerns in their business operations and in their interaction with their stakeholders on a voluntary basis'. (www://ec.europa.eu/enterprise/policies/sustainable-business/corporate-social-responsibility/index_en.htm) I believe it should be mandatory and extended to Individual Social Responsibility (ISR).

13. The Boston Consulting Group Matrix is a chart that was first created by Bruce Henderson for the Boston Consulting Group in 1968 to help corporations analyse business units or product lines with respect to market share (relative to competition) and market growth. Each product is placed in one of the four cells in the matrix: either stars (high growth market and high market share), questions marks (low share in high profit markets, cost hungry and little return), cash cows (high share of a low growth market, they generate more money than you invest) and dogs (low shares of low growth markets) that cost you money and you need to be eliminated. (www.bcg.com/about_bcg/history/history_1968.aspx)

5 DIFFERENTIATE

1. In an interview with Victor-M. Amela in *La Vanguardia* (20 May 2009) Rahaf Harfoush, strategist of the e-campaign of Barack Obama, talked about insights and her book *Yes We Did*.

2. To leverage a brand means to increase, or even better, to multiply the product's perceived value to potential customers to sell more.

3. According to Interbrand's guide to the most valuable brands, Google jumped from position ten in 2008 to seven in 2009, with a 25% change in brand value to $34,864 million. This growth has been justified largely by Google's continued business diversification and innovation. (www.interbrand.com/best_global_brands.aspx)

4. Chris Anderson, *The Long Tail* (Hyperion Books, 2006). The updated 2008 edition of this book includes a new chapter entitled 'The Long Tail of Marketing'.

5. Product life cycle is a basic concept to understand where a product comes from, its development, introduction, growth and maturity to decline. My point here is that there is no difference between a brand product or a non-branded product. Both will end up communicating and trying to create trust and confidence to guarantee further growth.

6. Checkpoint Charlie was a symbol of the Cold War: it was the best-known crossing point of the Berlin Wall dividing East Germany and West Germany. I have often mentally compared it to 'point of sale' (PoS). Whatever you have planned to do before reaching the PoS, this is where the customer takes the final buying decisions.

7. I can understand why many consumers are disappointed by over-promise or just really bad brands and their products or services. I could easily write a couple of books on brand experiences without substance, style, conviction and grace!

8. Consumer touch points are all points where the consumer is in contact with the company or the brand.

Thanks

Creating and growing go hand in hand. It is so true. This book has been created around my experience and ideas, but also with inspiration and feedback from the people around me over the last two decades – and more.

My parents Otto and Ilse gave me so many opportunities. One was to study design at the age of seventeen, not a usual choice back then. That turned out to be the starting point of a much longer journey, which I could not have made without my parents' trust and confidence. Studying design opened my heart and head to culture and art as well as design. Thanks so much for that. Here, too, I give my thanks to my wife Cari, who has supported me unconditionally and whose humorous creative inspiration and moral support ever since we met have brought so much to my life.

Special thanks to my Swedish ex-boss Peter Olsson (performanceplus.de), definitely one of the best players for celebrity marketing, for an intense but great time. And also special thanks to my Catalan ex-boss Jordi Mallol (globalhealthcare.es), an expert in pharmaceutical marketing and a great person, for his trust and confidence to work with me in Barcelona, thanks so much.

Then there are my students, each and every one an inspiring talent. I wish you all the very, very best and thank you for the time we have shared over the past seven years. That was made possible by the staff at IED (Istituto Europeo di Design) Barcelona, whose support also allowed me to develop this book and made life there much easier.

At various stages of writing this book Jürgen Aigner, Shazeela Ali, Carolina Amiguet, Jascha Blobel, Luis Felipe Guzman Vargas, Frank Gremmelspacher, Berta Loran, Zakir Maqsood, Marcos

Segador and Frederic Westerberg revised the manuscript. All of them had many other things to do with their time, but found the space to give me advice and input that I took very seriously. Many, many thanks to you all.

And then, of course, Vicky Hayward, my editor, the essential part of this growth process, who brought experience, insights, inspirations, reflections and patience to the work on the book. We spent hours on the phone, even before she had drunk her morning coffee. Thank you very much, Vicky.

During the writing of the book I had the luck to meet Simon Hüsler, who designed it and contributed his sharp-eyed graphics. He is one of those rare designers who read your mind and think ahead, challenging complex concepts and analysing them visually. It was a great experience to work with him. Thanks so much for all you brought to the book.

I do not want to forget Valeria de Luca and Marc-Alexander Baier, who helped me to market the book and communicate its message with enthusiasm and dedication.

At the Frankfurt Book Fair in 2012 I met Rudolf van Wetzel of BIS Publishers. This second revised edition has happened thanks to his openness to the book's ideas. I deeply appreciate his creative collaboration in taking this book to new markets and a far wider readership.

When I write I often have in mind my family. I hope that one day my cousins Axel, Meike and Johanna, and my godchildren, Lilly and Heidi, might read this book and find in it inspiration and new points of view. This book is for you all. Finally my thoughts turn to Dino Klein, a very special friend, who taught me a lot about life. I miss him so much, but he will always be in my heart.

Jürgen Salenbacher, Barcelona, February 2013

ABOUT THE AUTHOR

Jürgen Salenbacher is an independent lecturer, teacher and coach whose Creative Personal Branding workshops are taught internationally. The workshops bring together his knowledge and experience, acquired during twenty years' work, in branding, personal assessment and skill-sharing to support social change.

Salenbacher, born in 1970, began his career as an art director in Munich, Germany after studying design in Freiburg. While working in advertising he took a Public Relations diploma at the Bayerische Akademie der Werbung (BAW) in Munich. In the years that followed he travelled the world, working in design, marketing and communications. His experience in positioning local and world brands, personalities and even nations is unique. Clients have included Munich Aids Help Charity and Bayer Healthcare, Coca-Cola, Durex play, Levi's, Lego, Louis Vuitton, Mattel, Novartis, adidas international, Roca, Swatch and Vittel.

He had the opportunity to work on marketing and branding strategies for, among others, Michael Ballack, Muhammad Ali and Paolo Coelho and for the Kingdom of Bhutan. Awards include the red dot award, the New York Festival, the IPA Best of Health and the Art Directors' Club.

His Creative Personal Branding workshops (www.cpb-lab.com) were born after his work moved towards innovation and the creative economy. In 1997 he co-founded the creative agency D-Office, taking the role of Managing Director. In 2002 he was appointed Director of Marketing for The Performers (Omnicom Group), a leading agency for celebrities, sponsorship and venues. In 2005, after finishing an MBA at EADA Business School in Barcelona, he joined Global Healthcare, DDB's health agency in Spain, as Director of Strategy. In 2011, after teaching at the Design University IED Barcelona for five years, he was appointed as its Academic Director. He also coaches and teaches at HSLU in Luzern and Hyper Island in Stockholm.

He lives with his wife in Barcelona, enjoying tennis – which he coached professionally when younger – and the beach. Other interests include art, design, fashion, architecture, photography and travel. He is currently working on an essay about design education and his second book on creative leadership.

A SHORT BOOKLIST

Anderson, Chris, LONG TAIL, Hyperion, New York, 2006
Wired's editor-in-chief knows what he is talking about. The economy is changing and connectivity is key. Really key in understanding how marketing is changing.

Arden, Paul, IT'S NOT HOW GOOD YOU ARE, IT'S HOW GOOD YOU WANT TO BE, Phaidon Press, London, 2003
Easy to read wisdom by one of the best ever creative thinkers.

Baskin, Merry and Earls, Mark, BRAND NEW BRAND THINKING, Kogan Page Ltd, London, 2002
A sophisticated take on brand thinking written by members of the Account Planning Group in England – all practitioners. I recommend it to every current or future account or strategic planner.

Bronson, Po, WHAT SHOULD I DO WITH MY LIFE?, Ballantine Books, New York, 2005
Always a good question. Po Bronson describes the answer from people from all walks of life.

Burlingham, Bo, SMALL GIANTS, Penguin, New York, 2007
Great business book about companies that decided not to grow or sell-out, just to stay where they are and do a great job. Amazing, especially in comparison to all other growth-obsessed books.

Carlson, David, MAKE DESIGN BETTER, BIS Publishers, Amsterdam 2012
This book will help you to design better... and to make design matter!

Chan Kim, W. and Mauborgne, Renée, BLUE OCEAN STRATEGY, Harvard Business Press, Boston, 2005
One of the last decade's key books on strategy.

Clausewitz, Carl von, ON WAR, Princeton University Press, Princeton, 1989
A must-read if you develop strategies professionally. It is also interesting to understand the similarity between business and war.

De Bono, Edward, SIMPLICITY, Penguin Putnam, New York, 1998
As all of his books are worth reading, I choose this one because I am always interested in simplicity.

Denning, Stephen, LEADER'S GUIDE TO STORYTELLING, Jossey-Bass, London, 2005
A great book about the history of storytelling and its importance for leaders and leadership.

Frankl, Viktor E., MAN'S SEARCH FOR MEANING, Beacon Press, Boston, 2006
Deep understanding of motivation. Not easy to digest, but if you are asking yourself about life's most important questions then I believe this book will influence some of your ideas.

Gobé, Marc, EMOTIONAL BRANDING Allworth Press, New York, 2001
A great book about the importance of emotional connections between brands and their consumers.

Hara, Kenya, DESIGNING DESIGN, Lars Müller Verlag, Baden, 2007 (2nd edition)
Incredibly thoughtful and amazingly interesting. The author is the only person I know who is able to write pages about the concept of the colour white and able to explain Japanese design explicitly. On top of that it is a beautiful book.

Howkins, John, CREATIVE ECONOMY, Penguin Global, New York, 2002
Fundamental in understanding the importance of creative industries and their spin-off importance. Well researched. I use it as a key book to support work on talent development and education.

Kelley, Tom, TEN FACES OF INNOVATION, Profile Books, London, 2008
The CEO of IDEO has enough top cases and stories in this book for you to love it.

McCormack, Mark H., WHAT THEY DON'T TEACH YOU AT HARVARD BUSINESS SCHOOL, Bantam, New York, 1986
Mark McCormack, probably the most powerful man ever in sports business, the founder of IMG (International Management Group), shares his secrets about

serious sales, negotiating, time-management, decision-making and communication. Street-wise and hands-on.

Neumeier, Marty, BRAND GAP, New Riders Press, Berkeley, 2003
Mandatory reading for anyone working on brands and fun for others. It's easy to read, straight to the point and makes a complicated topic easy to understand. Beside that I like the visual examples.

O'Connor, Joseph and Lages, Andrea, COACHING WITH NLP, Element, Shaftesbury, 2004
If you are interested to have a good overview of what is coaching and what it is not, that's a good one.

Pink, Daniel H., A WHOLE NEW MIND, Riverhead Books, New York, 2005
Good for everyone uneasy in their careers, entrepreneurs and especially for those whose abilities have often been overlooked and undervalued. I love the description of the conceptual age as it reflects the creative economy.

Ridley, Matt, ORIGINS OF VIRTUE, Penguin, London, 1998
Matt Ridley explains how the human mind has evolved a special instinct for social exchange. Another great insight into human behaviour.

Sharma, Robin S., THE MONK WHO SOLD HIS FERRARI, HarperOne, London, 1999
A great book about personal change, good for any workaholic.

Sharp, Daryl, PERSONALITY TYPES, JUNG'S MODEL OF TYPOLOGY, Inner City Books, Toronto, 1987
If you deal with groups, in business or other areas, then I highly recommend this book to gain basic insights into how and why people are moved to act and react in so different ways.

Stickdorn, Marc and Schneider, Jakob, THIS IS SERVICE DESIGN THINKING, BIS Publisher, Amsterdam, 2012
The boundaries between products and services are blurring and it is time for a different way of thinking: this is service design thinking.

THE NEW YORKER 'THE INNOVATOR ISSUE' May 11, 2009

Awesome essays, especially Malcolm Gladwell's 'How David Beats Goliath' where he describes how David can beat Goliath by substituting effort for ability – and this formula turns to be the winning formular for underdogs. Just great.

Tybout, Alice M. and Calkins, Tim, KELLOGG ON BRANDING, Wiley, London, 2005

The academic book on branding. I would suggest dipping into it as the content is good, but sometimes exhausting.